Author's Business and Financial Handbook

Tips for Bookkeeping, Accounting, and Taxes
Ashley Guion, CPA, MSA

LIBRA LIBROS LLC

Contents

I'm an accountant, but not <u>your</u> accountant. Please contact a local professional that is knowledgeable about your specific situation (especially if you're not US based). The content in this book will be as US-based, and as generic as possible.

So, again, ***I'm not your CPA*** and ***I'm also not a lawyer***. **I'm also human and can make mistakes.** Use the enclosed information for discussion and independent research purposes. See the Disclosure Reminder for full disclosure

The more complex areas of this handbook have been marked with a * on their chapter titles. I highly recommend consulting with your own advisor about any (all) of these topics.

Disclosure Reminder

The information contained in this book is not intended to provide any tax or legal advice, and cannot be used for the purpose of avoiding tax penalties that may be imposed by the IRS.

By reading this book, you understand that this is an expression of opinions and not professional advice and will hold all members harmless in any event or claim. Under no circumstances will any blame or legal responsibility be held against the publisher, or author, for any damages, reparations, or monetary loss due to the information contained within this book. Either directly or indirectly.

By reading this document, the reader agrees that under no circumstances is the author responsible for any losses, direct or indirect, which are incurred as a result of the use of information contained within this book, including but not limited to: errors, omissions, or inaccuracies.

This is not a substitute for working with a tax professional. This information is for general discussion purposes only.

The information provided is general US tax law – no states included.

The interpretation of tax laws may vary among different preparers, and your own tax professional might have a different perspective. It's essential to recognize that individual interpretations can differ, and the interpretation of the information provided here may not align with everyone's understanding. Even though the content has been reviewed by myself and another CPA, we are all human, and errors (and misinterpretations) may still occur (though obviously I did my best to avoid them :-)).

Given the dynamic nature of tax laws, it's important to note that regulations are always changing. Every tax situation is different, and you should talk to your own tax professional to make sure you are claiming income and expenses according to your specific situation. Stay informed about updates in tax laws that might affect your financial strategies.

Any reliance you place on this information is at your own risk. The author and publisher disclaim all liability for any loss, damage, or inconvenience caused by reliance on the information presented within this book. The goal is to empower authors with knowledge, but readers are urged to exercise due diligence and verify information in their specific context.

Did I say it enough times yet? Do you get my point? Use this as a *guide*, not as your *rulebook*. The intention is to provide helpful insights/interpretations, but remember, your financial landscape is unique. Consult with your tax professional to navigate your individual journey. This book serves as a compass, not a rigid map.

This handbook is up-to-date as of the 12/31/23 tax law

Please make sure that any of the tax or business information hasn't changed before considering implementing anything discussed

There are some topics discussed that are probably more advanced than most of you want to get into and that's totally fine. I tried not to get *too* technical in some of those more complex areas but the information is there if you want it...and now when your accountant says certain keywords, they won't be completely foreign to you (or at least you can run home, pull out this book, and see what the heck they were talking about :-)) **I starred those more complex topics with " * " in the chapter title**

CHAPTER 1

Understanding the Necessity of This Book

Welcome to your ultimate financial companion tailored specifically for authors.

This book is designed with _you_ in mind – someone passionate about storytelling but seeking clarity and control over the financial side of your writing business.

As a CPA-turned-author, I'm dedicated to leveraging my extensive experience and training from the financial world to assist fellow writers, ensuring that my expertise contributes meaningfully to my writing community.

Why *This* Handbook And Not Another?

Accessible, Non-Financial Language:
- Dive into a world where financial concepts are demystified

- I've crafted each chapter using simple, relatable language, ensuring that even the most complex financial concepts become digestible and easy to understand for non-finance brains

Bite-Sized and Skim-Friendly:
- Embrace the freedom to navigate

- Each section is broken down into bite-sized, skim-able chunks

- Dive deep or skim through; this book empowers you to seek the information you need, precisely when you need it

Practical Application for Authors:

- Find immediate solutions to your financial concerns

- Every chapter addresses real-world scenarios encountered by authors, offering practical advice and actionable steps to address your financial pain points

  - This is no generic 'accounting and business for small business owners' handbook – this is catered _to_ authors, _by_ an author.

User-Centric Navigation:
- Discover a book that fits into your lifestyle

- Whether you're a busy writer on the go or prefer dedicated reading sessions, the user-friendly structure enables seamless navigation and quick access to relevant information

Why Do _You_ Need This Handbook?

Financial Empowerment:
- Many authors overlook the business side of their craft, focusing solely on writing

- Understanding the financial landscape empowers you to navigate your author career with confidence

- Proper accounting and bookkeeping can help you drop the pen names/series/platforms that are resulting in unnecessary losses and pivot to expand the successful offerings

Long-term Sustainability:
- Establishing a solid financial structure secures the longevity of your writing career

- It's not just about the next book; it's about building a sustainable and thriving business

Risk Mitigation:
- Weak financial strategies/knowledge can expose you to unnecessary risks

- Identifying and rectifying these weaknesses is crucial to safeguarding your livelihood as an author

What This Book Can Do For *You*

Provide Clarity:
- We will demystify financial concepts and present them in a manner easily understood by authors, irrespective of financial background.

Offer Practical Solutions:
- I'll present actionable steps and solutions tailored to authors, addressing your specific financial pain points and offering strategies for improvement (always consult with a local professional to confirm that the steps are right for you. It will be a lot less expensive if you have a rough understanding beforeh there is less time spent on discussion with them)

- CPAs are usually billed out in six minute increments. In my area of the US, we're billed out at $200/hr+. Scan this handbook to get a grasp on the basics, *and then*, reach out to your accountant for more specifics/applicability.

  ○ Save yourself some $$

  ○ Also, put the purchase price of this handbook under 'office expense'. Yay deductions!

Support Your Creative Journey:
- By addressing financial weaknesses, I aim to alleviate stress, allowing you to focus on what you do best—telling captivating stories

Conclusion:

- Embrace a newfound sense of financial empowerment without the overwhelm.

- **This book is your go-to resource, inviting you to explore financial management in a way that's approachable, adaptable, and tailored to your unique journey as an author**

No more nerves—you got this

CHAPTER 2
The Beauty of Accounting

Accounting is like creating a story with numbers instead of words.

It helps you understand the financial story of your writing business.

Just like a plot needs structure, accounting organizes your income, expenses, and other financial details.

It's your guide to knowing how much money you're making, where it's coming from, and where it's going.

This helps you make smart decisions, plan for the future, and keep your writing journey on track

CHAPTER 3

Cash vs. Accrual Basis Accounting

In accounting, businesses usually report their financial activities using either the cash or accrual basis.

Cash basis accounting tracks transactions based on when money physically enters or leaves the business. It's straightforward—you record income when you receive payment and expenses when you make payments.

Accrual basis accounting, on the other hand, logs transactions when they occur, regardless of when the money actually exchanges hands. This method matches revenues with the expenses incurred to generate them, giving a more comprehensive view of the business's financial health.

Choosing between these methods depends on the needs of the business and the reporting standards it follows.

However, as authors, most of us are probably cash basis.

Regardless, here is the high-level comparison:

- **Cash Basis Accounting:**

    ○ Records transactions when cash is received or paid.

    ○ Income and expenses are recognized only when money changes hands.

    ○ Simple and straightforward for tracking actual cash flow.

- **Accrual Basis Accounting:**

    ○ Reflects a more accurate financial position by matching revenues and expenses.

    ○ Records income when earned and expenses when incurred, regardless of cash flow.

    - For instance, a sale might be recorded in one accounting period but the payment might be received in a subsequent period, impacting the timing of recognizing revenue. Understanding these concepts is crucial for accurately depicting the financial health and performance of a business, especially for authors managing their book-related income and expenses.

- Example: You may earn $5,000 in royalties on Amazon in December, however, you aren't paid for those royalties until the following year. A cash-basis reporter, would include those December royalties paid in the next year, <u>in</u> the next year. An accrual-basis tax payer would record those royalties earned in December, <u>in</u> December.

  - Why this is important? Say you paid $3,000 in ad spend in December, if you're looking at your income statement on a month to month basis, if you're accrual, you see the $5,000 in royalties and the $3,000 in spend, matching the revenue to the incurred expense. If you're cash basis, you might see only $2,000 in revenues deposited in December and mistakenly think that the ad spend was a bust. So, even though I'm not saying that you should try to be accrual, from a business advisor standpoint, it is important to keep track of those types of timing differences when evaluating and making decisions/conclusions

CHAPTER 4

Ratios

Ratios are essential because they offer insights into a business's financial health and operational efficiency (and lenders use them).

Why are ratios important?

Performance Evaluation:
- Ratios help assess how well a business is performing in various areas like profitability, liquidity, solvency, and efficiency.

  ○ They provide a means to compare current performance against past performance or industry benchmarks.

Decision Making:
- They aid in decision-making processes for management, investors, and creditors.

  ○ By analyzing ratios, stakeholders can make informed decisions about investments, lending, operational changes, or future strategies.

Identifying Trends:
- Ratios can reveal trends over time.

  ○ Consistent analysis allows for the identification of patterns or shifts in the company's financial position, indicating areas of strength or weakness.

Communication Tool:
- They serve as a common language for communication about financial health.

  ○ Investors, lenders, and internal stakeholders can quickly grasp a company's status through these metrics.

Early Warning Signals:
- Some ratios act as early warning signals for potential financial problems.

○ For instance, deteriorating liquidity ratios may indicate future cash flow issues.

Common Ratios

Current Ratio:
- Calculated by dividing current assets by current liabilities.

- Indicates a business's ability to cover its short-term liabilities with its short-term assets.

- A ratio above 1 suggests the business can meet its short-term obligations.

Quick Ratio (Acid-Test Ratio):
- Similar to the current ratio but excludes inventory from current assets.

- If we assume that authors aren't carrying significant inventory – this one will generate the same results as Current Ratio above

- It measures a company's ability to pay off short-term liabilities without relying on selling inventory.

Return on Assets (ROA):
- This ratio shows how effectively a company utilizes its assets to generate profit by comparing net income to total assets.

Operating Cash Flow Ratio:
- This ratio measures a company's ability to generate cash from its operations, comparing operating cash flow to total debt.

There are many, many more, but these a few of the most common. You can find more online.

CHAPTER 5

Starting Your Writing Business

You might just be starting out and wondering where to begin, here are a few key steps (discussed more later as well).

Define Your Niche:
- Determine your writing focus—fiction, non-fiction, genres, or specific themes you're passionate about.

Market Research and Niche Definition:
- Understand your target audience, identify market trends, and define your niche within the writing industry.

Create a Business Plan:
- Outline your goals, target audience, marketing strategies, and revenue streams.
- This plan will serve as a roadmap for your writing business.

Legal Structure:
- Choose a business structure—sole proprietorship, single-member LLC, multi-member LLC, partnership, S-Corporation, or C Corporation.
- Each has different legal and tax implications.

Register Your Business:
- File necessary paperwork with your local government to register your business.
- Obtain any required licenses or permits.

<u>Separate ALL Finances:</u>
- **Open a <u>separate</u> bank account for your writing income and expenses to keep personal and business finances distinct (Also, if you can, do a separate PayPal, Square, email, etc. Trust me – don't cross the streams unless you're putting money into the business or taking money out.)**
  - Set it up correctly right from the start.

- What's the phrase? *If you don't have time to do it right, when will you have time to do it over?*

- Do yourself a favor and set yourself up for success. Keep those money funnels separate!

  ○ It will make tax prep much easier as well!

- Some entity types actually require separation of the accounts, so just assume the same goes for you and do it.

  ○ Find a no-fee checking account somewhere and thank me later.

Set Up Accounting Systems:
- Establish an accounting system to track income, expenses, miles driven, home office, and taxes.

  ○ Depending on your level of activity, you could:

    - Use a paper system *(hey, I have a log book for that – check it out online)*

    - Use a spreadsheet for tracking (Excel, Sheets, etc) *(I have an awesome spreadsheet – look that up as well)*

    - Use a software (QuickBooks Online, Xero, etc) *(I personally use QBO because I love automation and less data entry)*

    - Or hire a Bookkeeper, etc

Build an Online Presence:
- Create an author website, social media profiles, and author platforms to showcase your work and connect with readers.

Network:
- Engage with other authors, join writing groups, attend literary events, etc

  ○ Remember, if this is going to be your business, act like it.

    - How you present yourself online... it's important...I don't need to explain the importance of this, right?

  ○ Keep track of those miles driven

Marketing Strategy:
- Devise a marketing strategy encompassing branding, online presence development (website, social media), book launch plans, and promotional tactics.

- Research what the required disclosures are for email footers, international laws regarding data privacy, and any terms and conditions that may need to be added to your website.

Start Writing:
- Begin creating content!

  ○ Whether it's novels, articles, blogs, or short stories, start producing the material that represents your brand as a writer.

- Align your content with your identified niche and audience preferences.

  ○ From a business advisor standpoint, I caution against genre hopping until you have a solid base under one pen name, but it's your business–do what you want.

Intellectual Property Protection:
- Research copyright for your literary works, explore trademarking your brand, and understand intellectual property rights for your creations.

- Assess whether you want/need to formally copyright your product.

Sales and Distribution Channels:
- Plan your book distribution strategy, considering options like online retailers, local bookstores, direct sales, or self-publishing platforms.

Retirement accounts:
- Once you start turning a profit, please don't forget to pay yourself a retirement.

  ○ So many of my self-employed clients are reluctant to part with the cash to fund retirement accounts (discussed later), but remember, you don't have an employer dropping retirement funds in an account for you

  ○ the time and space in your budget to do this.

  ○ Don't turn seventy-years-old and only have your royalty income and social security.

Additional Considerations:
- Consider aspects like business insurance, legal compliance, professional services for legal and financial advice, intellectual property rights management, operational organization tips, and financial planning to ensure a well-rounded and successful writing business.

  ○ **A note on self-employment taxes** – when you work for someone else as a W2 employee, the employer withholds a portion of your income to cover your payroll tax obligations and then remits that to the governmental agencies. The employer also has to pay their 50% in payroll taxes on your income. But when you are self-employed, you pay the employer and employee portions of Social Security and Medicare taxes.

- This 15.3% of self-employment tax is calculated on your business income, on top of your ordinary income tax rate

- This calculation of self-employment taxes is calculated at the same time as you prepare your Form 1040 personal income tax return

- Generally, the government wants estimated tax payments made throughout the year to spread out this tax liability. See my notes in later sections.

These steps collectively lay the groundwork for establishing a thriving writer/author business, balancing creative endeavors with essential business practices.

CHAPTER 6

Accounting, Bookkeeper, CPA, EA, Tax Preparer

Each of these professionals plays a distinct role in managing financial and tax-related aspects for their clients, with differences in their expertise, certifications, and the breadth of services they can offer.

Depending on the complexity of your financial situation or business needs, choosing the right professional can ensure comprehensive guidance and support in managing your financial affairs and tax obligations.

Accountant:

- An accountant is a financial professional responsible for managing and interpreting financial records.

- They analyze financial data, prepare reports, and provide insights that help individuals or organizations make informed financial decisions.

- Accountants often hold degrees in accounting or finance and may have certifications like CPA (Certified Public Accountant) or CMA (Certified Management Accountant).

- They handle tasks like financial statement preparation, tax planning, auditing, and advising on various financial matters.

- They can do anything a bookkeeper does, but they may offer more guidance on financial matters

Bookkeeper:

- A bookkeeper is primarily focused on recording and organizing financial transactions.

- They maintain accurate records of income and expenses, reconcile accounts, and ensure that financial data is properly categorized and recorded.

- Bookkeepers may not hold advanced degrees but have expertise in using accounting software and maintaining day-to-day financial records.

- Their role is essential in providing organized and accurate financial data for accountants or CPAs to analyze and use in financial reporting and decision-making processes.

Certified Public Accountants (CPAs):

- Certified Public Accountants have a broader scope compared to EAs.

- They are licensed by states and can specialize in various areas within accounting, offering a wider range of services beyond tax-related matters.

- CPAs can work as auditors, financial planners, corporate accountants, tax consultants, and more.

- They possess expertise in accounting, tax, financial planning, and advisory services for businesses, individuals, and various other organizations.

- CPAs can represent clients in IRS matters and provide comprehensive financial guidance, including tax planning and compliance.

- Me :-)

Enrolled Agents (EAs):

- Enrolled Agents are specialized tax professionals recognized by the IRS.

- They hold the highest credential awarded *by the IRS*, focusing specifically on managing tax arrangements for businesses or individuals.

- EAs are knowledgeable about federal tax laws and regulations, making them adept at handling tax-related matters, including preparation, representation, and advising on tax-related issues before the IRS.

Tax Preparers:

- Tax Preparers, unlike EAs or CPAs, do not require specific designations or certifications.

- They specialize in preparing tax returns for individuals or businesses.

- They are hired to assist clients with tax-related paperwork, ensuring accurate and compliant tax filings.

CHAPTER 7

Hobby vs. Self—Employment Income

Understanding the difference between hobby income and self-employment income is crucial for tax purposes.

The IRS distinguishes between activities pursued primarily for personal enjoyment and those conducted for profit.

This distinction greatly impacts how income is reported and the deductions you can claim.

Hobby Income:

- Income generated from an activity that is pursued for pleasure, recreation, or enjoyment rather than for profit.

- Where to report hobby income:

  - If the IRS considers an author's writing activities as a hobby rather than a business, any income generated is reported on your **Form 1040 on Schedule 1, line 8j**

- Where to report hobby expenses:

  - As of this writing, the IRS does not allow deductions for hobby expenses. Therefore it is impossible to have hobby losses.

Self—Employment Income:

- Income derived with the intention of making a profit and conducting their writing endeavors in a business-like manner.

- Where to report self-employment income:

  - Self-employment income from writing books, freelance writing, or related activities is reported on **Schedule C (Profit or Loss from Business) of Form 1040.**

  - If you are a multi-member LLC, partnership, S-corp, (or even C-corp) – that's handled differently.

- Where to report self-employment expenses:

  - Authors can deduct business expenses from their self-employment income, reducing their taxable income

  - Self-employment business expenses related to writing activities, such as office expenses, marketing costs, research materials, and more are reported on Schedule C (Profit or Loss from Business) of Form 1040

    - Again, if you are a multi-member LLC, partnership, S-corp, (or even C-corp) – that's handled differently.

Determining Factors:

- It's crucial for authors to accurately determine whether their writing activities qualify as a business or a hobby according to IRS guidelines.

- Keeping detailed records, maintaining a separate business bank account, having a business plan, actively seeking to make a profit, and demonstrating business-like behavior can help support the classification of writing activities as self-employment income rather than hobby income.

- **Three-out-of-five-years test**

  - There's an IRS guidelines commonly known as the "three-out-of-five-years test" for determining whether an activity is engaged in for profit, especially in the context of businesses or activities that might initially generate losses.

  - According to this guideline, if a business or activity, such as an author's writing endeavors, incurs losses for three or more out of five consecutive tax years (including the current year and the prior four years), the *IRS <u>might</u> scrutinize whether the activity is truly engaged in for profit or if it's a hobby.*

- **It's essential to note that meeting this test <u>is not the sole determinant of whether an activity is considered a business or hobby for tax purposes.</u> Don't let the rumor mill in social media spaces steer you differently.**

  - The IRS evaluates various factors beyond this test, considering the author's effort to make a profit, business-like behavior, expertise, and other relevant circumstances.

- Authors aiming to treat their writing as a business should keep detailed records, maintain a profit motive, and demonstrate efforts to improve profitability over time to substantiate their business intent and meet IRS guidelines.

  - I believe it also helps to keep business records separate from personal records (get that separate credit card, open that business checking account, separate the PayPal or Venmo accounts. Don't pierce the metaphorical *corporate veil*. Act as if it's a business – because it is.)

CHAPTER 8

*Entity Selection & Associated Tax Forms

Choosing the right business entity is a fundamental decision that can significantly impact your business's operations, legal structure, tax obligations, and personal liability.

Each business structure—sole proprietorship, single-member LLC, multi-member LLC, partnership, S Corporation, C Corporation—offers distinct advantages and disadvantages.

Understanding these differences is crucial in establishing a business that aligns with your goals, financial strategy, and risk tolerance.

I do try to give basic entity formation tips though, you should also confirm with a local attorney or business bureau about the requirements in your area
(as I'm not legal counsel, this is <u>very</u> generic formation advice. Double check your local requirements).

Let's explore the unique characteristics of each business entity to help you (and your advisors) make an informed choice for your writing venture.

CHAPTER 9

Sole Proprietors & Single-Member Limited Liability Companies (SMLLC)

Sole Proprietorship:

- A sole proprietorship is the simplest form of business organization, where an individual operates the business as the sole owner.

- In this structure, the business and its owner are legally considered the same entity.

- **Key Feature:**

  - The direct reporting of business income and losses on the owner's personal tax return.

- **Pros and Cons:**

  - **Pros:**

    - Offers simplicity and economy in formation and operation *(and is usually the easiest way for new authors to start out)*

  - **Cons:**

    - The owner's unlimited personal liability for any business debts or obligations, including any liabilities created by an employee

Single-Member Limited Liability Company (SMLLC):

- A Single-Member Limited Liability Company (SMLLC) is a legal entity that offers limited liability protection to its single owner (member)

- **Key Feature:**

  - This structure combines the flexibility of a sole proprietorship with limited liability protection, shielding the member's personal assets from business liabilities (to an extent – see the note later), and from claims resulting from liabilities created by an employee.

  - This will be operated under the taxpayer's social security number (or other tax identification number if they don't have an SSN)

- **Pros and Cons:**

  - **Pros**:

    - SMLLCs provide limited liability protection, safeguarding the owner's personal assets from business liabilities (to an extent – see the note later)

  - **Cons**:

    - Additional administrative requirements compared to a sole proprietorship.

    - Some states make it really easy/inexpensive, others are more complicated/expensive

      - *Check with your state about things like annual reporting requirements, fees, etc.*

Distinguishing Between Sole Proprietorship and Single-Member LLC:

- The primary distinction lies in liability protection and legal structure.

  - Both are rather simple, but an SMLLC provides a separation between personal and business liabilities that a sole proprietorship lacks.

- Federal tax reporting forms are the same

Steps to Create a Sole Proprietorship or Single-Member LLC:

This is not an exhaustive list – please check with your local regulations

Sole Proprietorship Formation:

- **Choosing a Business Name:**

  - Select a name that aligns with your business vision and ensure it's not already in use by another entity, which you can often determine through your state's online name registry.

  - Also, check local business registries and domain availability to verify its uniqueness.

- **Registration and Compliance:**

  - Registering a sole proprietorship usually involves less formalities, but ensure compliance with local regulations, such as whether you can operate as a home-based business in your local zoning district.

  - Obtain any necessary licenses or permits mandated by your industry or jurisdiction.

- **Tax ID (EIN):**

  - While not always required for sole proprietors without employees, obtaining an Employer Identification Number (EIN) *can* facilitate separation of personal and business finances.

    - Though, you may find that banks or book distributors such as Amazon will still require your SSN rather than the FEIN given that the IRS views this as a 'disregarded entity'

  - Some states may require their own state EIN – do your research

- **Business Address:**

  - Consider setting up a business address separate from your home address for a professional image, or if you're not permitted to operate a business from your residence.

    - Many lawyers will allow themselves to be listed as 'registered agents' and will allow any formal correspondence to go through them

    - Options include using a PO Box or obtaining a virtual business address service – can provide a bit more privacy – but double check the requirements as most states don't technically allow you to use a PO box

Single-Member LLC Formation:

- **Choosing a Unique Business Name:**

  ○ Select an original and distinguishable business name and verify its availability through a name search with the state's business registry, often searchable through the Secretary of State's office.

- **Tax ID (EIN):**

  ○ While not always mandatory for Single-Member LLCs (SMLLC) without employees, securing an Employer Identification Number (EIN) can be crucial for various tax purposes beyond the separation of personal and business finances.

    - It might be necessary for sales tax registration, Value Added Tax (VAT) compliance, foreign filings, and other tax obligations, especially if your business expands its operations, deals with international clients, or engages in interstate commerce.

    - Obtaining an EIN can streamline these processes and ensure compliance with diverse tax regulations.

      ○ Can be quickly, easily, and **freely** obtained online by going to irs.gov

  ○ Though, you may find that banks or book distributors such as Amazon will still require your SSN because SMLLCs are still considered 'disregarded entities'

  ○ Some states may require their own state EIN – do your research

- **Articles of Organization (if necessary):**

  ○ File a formation application with the state's Secretary of State or equivalent department.

  ○ Pay the requisite filing fees associated with the LLC formation.

- **Operating Agreement:**

  ○ Draft an operating agreement outlining the internal workings, management structure, and member responsibilities within the SMLLC.

  ○ This agreement establishes guidelines for decision-making processes, profit-sharing, and roles within the company.

- This agreement helps establish the LLC as separate from you personally

- **Obtaining Licenses and Permits:**

  ○ Ensure compliance by obtaining the necessary licenses, permits, or certifications for your business activities, varying based on your industry and location.

    - Check into sales tax requirements, if necessary. As well as Resale Certificate or Seller's Permits

    - Also check to see whether there are annual reporting requirements, as some states mandate this, as well as a payment, to keep the LLC in good standing.

- **Business Address:**

  ○ An SMLLC typically requires a registered office address for legal and official correspondence, which can be a physical address or a registered agent's address.

  ○ In some states this is public information on the Secretary of State's website.

    - Consider the idea of your home address being available to anyone/everyone

Taxes:

Sole Proprietorship <u>and</u> Single-Member LLC FEDERAL Taxation:

- **Reporting Income:**

  ○ Sole proprietors & Single-Member LLCs report business income and losses on Schedule C of their personal tax return (Form 1040).

    - In years of net income, you pay your ordinary income tax rate on the income, but you also pay self employment taxes on that business net income. Double ouch.

    - In years of net losses, you are (usually) able to take the loss amount on your tax return to offset other income sources

- **Self-Employment Taxes:**

  - Sole proprietors & SMLLC members are responsible for paying self-employment taxes (Social Security and Medicare taxes) on net business income.

  - This adds up to 15.3% on top of your regular income tax rate

  Look up information specific to your own state requirements

Tax Deadlines:

- As mentioned above, your tax return (Form 1040) including the business Schedule C forms, is due on April 15th (more or less) like usual.

  - There might also be a requirement to file state returns

    - Double check your state – you have no idea how many clients I have in New Hampshire that say "NH doesn't have an income tax, so I don't need to file there." Eeeeehhhhh. Wrong. NH may have no sales tax or income tax, but they have NH business taxes once you hit a certain threshold. *Check your particular state.*

  - We'll talk about income tax nexus and sales tax nexus later.

Quarterly Tax Obligations:

- As a sole proprietor or single-member LLC, you're *expected* to make quarterly estimated tax payments to the IRS based on your business income.

  - Quarterly tax obligations for sole proprietors or Single-Member LLCs differ from the typical W-2 employee structure. Instead of having taxes withheld from each paycheck, business owners are responsible for estimating and paying their taxes directly to the IRS on a quarterly basis.

    - The IRS will calculate your tax balance when you complete your taxes and then figure out what you should have paid in each quarter. They will assess interest and penalties on any underpayments

    - Therefore, when you're self-employed, the IRS is no longer receiving those payroll taxes, neither from the employer portion or the employee portion, and they like their payroll tax income. Quarterly estimates are their way of trying to encourage more cash flow to them during the year (in my opinion, though I'm sure there's a more elegant way to explain it)

- The IRS provides Form 1040-ES, which helps calculate these estimated payments based on your business income, deductions, and other factors.

- **Calculating Quarterly Payments:**

  - Payments are due in April, June, September, and January.

  - They're typically 25% of the estimated tax liability for that year.

  - Accurately estimating these payments is crucial to avoid underpayment penalties and interest charges levied by the IRS.

- **Penalties for Underpayments:**

  - The IRS may impose penalties and interest on underpaid quarterly taxes. These penalties vary based on the amount and duration of the underpayment.

- **A note:** This is not tax advice but I will mention it as I think it fosters good thought, especially for business owners in times of tight cash flow.

  - I've had a lot of very wealthy clients over the years. When they're sending in $50,000 per quarterly, they start to get a little testy. I've heard many of them say that they don't want to give the IRS an "interest-free loan for the year" and that they could make more in their stock market account than they would have to pay in underpayment interest and penalties. *They* were willing to pay those interest and penalties for the sake of keeping that money in their metaphorical pockets longer. Again, I'm not advising you to do so, I'm just pointing out, that as of right now, the IRS is not going to come seize your house, take your first born, kill your dog, and throw you in jail if you don't pay estimates throughout the year.

  - **Also, the IRS will not call you and tell you that you owe them money. Be very cautious if you receive one of those phone calls (or emails) because these are most likely scams. The IRS doesn't generally conduct business via those methods, as they usually only communicate in writing (letters).**

Tax impact on financial transactions between you and your business:

- **Any money you put in or take out of your sole-proprietor or SMLLC business is a nontaxable event to the IRS**

- In fact, you can't really even have loans between you and the business.

  - Instead, money you put in or take out is considered a 'contribution' or a 'draw'. *You* may intend to reimburse yourself for that 'loan' but in fact, it's not a loan and its just your 'contribution' to the business and then your 'draw' upon repayment.

    - The IRS doesn't even ask what you put in or took out of the business during the year.

    - You could have a net income on your Schedule C return of $50,000 and the IRS doesn't care if you left all of that money still sitting in your business bank account —> you're still going to get taxed on that net income even though you took out none of it.

      - Conversely, in the following year, if you have that $50,000 cash sitting in your business checking and you take it all out to pay yourself as 'draw,' (not an expense!) and then at the end of the year, you had a huge net loss (again, not counting that draw that you took out), the IRS has you report the net loss on your income tax return, regardless of the fact that you pulled $50,000 from the business checking. They don't even know that you took a draw of $50,000. As far as they're concerned, you took it all in the year you earned it. I hope that makes sense.

- See Additional Considerations for more details

Common Pitfalls:

- **Commingling Funds**:

  - Avoid mixing personal and business finances, as this could jeopardize limited liability protection for an SMLLC and create complications during tax audits.

- After all, if you disregard your personal and LLC separation, it will be easier for creditors to do so as well. Then, you will have lost the primary advantage of using an LLC in the first place, which was to limit your personal liability.

- **<u>Wages:</u>** <u>As a sole proprietor or single-member LLC, you are NOT an "employee"</u>

  - You cannot take a W2 paycheck from your business, but instead can withdraw profits, known as a "draw," but these draws aren't considered a business expense or deduction.

  - You still get taxed on the net income of the business, whether you took the money out of the business checking or not.

  - You can just withdraw money from the business checking account tax-free. Record it as an owner's draw just so you know what it was for when you look at your finances, but you don't need to do anything more than that. It's as easy as that

CHAPTER 10

Partnership & Multi-Member Limited Liability Company (LLC)

Partnerships:

- A partnership involves two or more individuals sharing ownership and management responsibilities for a business.

- This structure allows partners to combine their resources, skills, and expertise to run the business together.

- **Key Features:**

  - **Ownership and Liability:**

    - Partners share ownership, profits, and liabilities, which can extend to personal assets.

  - **Types:**

    - Partnerships can be general partnerships (GPs) or limited partnerships (LPs), differing in partner liability and management involvement.

      - My comments below deal primarily with general partnerships, but an attorney can clarify further

- **Pros and Cons:**

  - **Pros:**

    - Partnerships offer shared responsibility, diverse skill sets, and flexibility in decision-making.

  - **Cons:**

    - Partners share personal liability for debts, and disagreements among partners can impact the business.

- **Important Notes:**

- **Legal Agreements:**

  - Drafting a partnership agreement is **<u>crucial</u>** to outline ownership percentages, profit distribution, decision-making, and conflict resolution processes.

    - Your tax preparer needs these numbers.

    - Nerdy fact: if you have two people who want to create a partnership together, one has the cash, and one has the expertise. From an accounting/tax standpoint, their contributions to the partnership **are not** equal. If you put in $50,000 and the other partner puts in $0.00, that will affect your capital/basis accounts. It won't affect your record keeping or anything, but I wanted to bring it up because it will affect how your partnership return K-1s may look different. Experience does not equal cash in the eyes of the IRS. If you have periods of sustained losses, you (who contributed $50k) may be able to claim those losses, while the 'muscle' who contributed $0, may be limited in claiming those deductions. Talk with your accountant.

- **Taxation:**

  - Partnerships file informational tax returns (Form 1065) but don't pay income tax themselves.

    - Instead, **profits and losses pass through to individual partners' tax returns (Schedule K-1).**

Multi-Member Limited Liability Companies (MMLLCs):

- A Multi-Member Limited Liability Company (MMLLC) involves multiple owners (*members*) sharing ownership and managerial responsibilities, similar to a partnership.

- **Key Features:**

  - **Limited Liability:** Members have limited liability protection, shielding personal assets from business liabilities, *including* from liabilities created by another member

  - **Flexibility:** MMLLCs offer flexibility in ownership structure, management, and profit distribution among multiple members.

    - <u>Please</u> specify the percentages of each in the Operating Agreement – it affects your taxes.

- **Pros and Cons**

  - **Pros:** Limited liability protection, flexibility in management, and pass-through taxation.

  - **Cons:** Additional administrative responsibilities compared to sole proprietorships.

- **Important Notes:**

  - **Operating Agreement:**

    - Draft an operating agreement detailing member rights, responsibilities, profit-sharing, and dispute resolution methods.

      - This is **<u>crucial</u> as it demonstrates that the LLC is being structured and operated on a business-like basis, which is critical for the avoidance of personal liability.**

  - **Taxation:**

    - Similar to partnerships, MMLLCs file informational tax returns (Form 1065), and members report their share of profits/losses on their individual tax returns (Schedule K-1).

Distinguishing Between Partnerships and MMLLCs:

- While both structures involve shared ownership and managerial responsibilities, MMLLCs offer limited liability protection to members, which partnerships typically do not provide.

- Federal tax reporting forms are the same

  - **Partnerships and MMLLCs file informational tax returns (Form 1065) to report business income, deductions, gains, and losses.**

    - But the tax responsibility ultimately passes through to individual partners or members.

  - **YOU <u>CANNOT</u> file your personal 1040 Tax Return UNTIL this Form 1065 is complete for the year.**

    - In English: The 1065 return creates a form (K-1) that has numbers on it that will drop into your personal tax return

Steps to Create a Partnership & MMLLC

(This is not an exhaustive list – please check with your local regulations. You'll also see that these are all very similar to each other)

Partnership Formation:

- **Choosing a Business Name:**

  - Select a name that aligns with your business vision and ensure it's not already in use by another entity, which you can often determine through your Secretary of State's online business name registry.

  - Check local business registries and domain availability to verify its uniqueness.

- **Registration and Compliance:**

  - File the necessary paperwork with the state to register the partnership.

  - Comply with local regulations, including obtaining licenses or permits required for the partnership's activities.

    - Also determine whether zoning approval is necessary if the partnership will be operating in a residential area.

- **Tax ID (EIN):**

  - **Obtain an Employer Identification Number (EIN) for the partnership.**

  - Some states may require their own state EIN – do your research

  - Regardless of whether your state requires its own EIN, you definitely need a federal EIN which you can get for free on irs.gov

- **Partnership Agreement:**

- Draft a comprehensive partnership agreement outlining ownership percentages, profit distribution, decision-making processes, dispute resolution methods, and each partner's rights and responsibilities.

  - You would be wise to have a lawyer at least review your agreement to ensure all important provisions are included.

- This agreement is crucial for clarity, setting expectations, and avoiding potential conflicts among partners.

- Give a copy to your accountant for their files.

- **Business Address:**

  - Decide on a business address separate from personal addresses for professional purposes, but again, if a residence is being used as the business office, check your local ordinances for compliance before going full-steam ahead.

    - Options *may* include a physical location, a registered agent, PO Box, or virtual business address service.

Multi-Member LLC Formation:

- **Choosing a Business Name:**

  - Select a name that aligns with your business vision and ensure it's not already in use by another entity, which you can often determine through your Secretary of State's online business name registry.

  - Check local business registries and domain availability to verify its uniqueness.

- **Registration and Compliance:**

  - File the necessary paperwork with the state to register the MMLLC.

  - Comply with local regulations, including obtaining licenses or permits required for the MMLLC's activities.

  - Also determine whether zoning approval is necessary if the MMLLC will be operating in a residential area.

- **Tax ID (EIN):**

  - **Obtain an Employer Identification Number (EIN) for the MMLLC.**

  - Some states may require their own state EIN – do your research

    - Regardless on whether your state requires its own EIN, you definitely need a federal EIN which you can get for free on irs.gov

- **Articles of Organization:**

  - File Articles of Formation with the state's Secretary of State or equivalent department.

  - Ensure to pay the required filing fees associated with this filing and determine whether annual reports and/or filing fees are necessary to keep the LLC in good standing.

- **Operating Agreement:**

  - Draft an operating agreement that outlines member rights, responsibilities, profit distribution, and management structures within the Multi-Member LLC.

    - You would be wise to have a lawyer at least review your agreement to ensure all important provisions are included.

  - Give a copy to your accountant for their files.

- **Licenses and Permits:**

  - Ensure compliance by obtaining any required licenses, permits, or certifications for your business activities. Requirements vary based on industry and location.

- **Business Address:**

  - An MMLLC typically requires a registered office address for legal and official correspondence, which can be a physical address or a registered agent's address.

    - Again, if a residence is being used as the business office, check your local ordinances for compliance before going full-steam ahead.

  - In some states this is public information on the Secretary of State's website.

    - Consider the idea of your home address being available to anyone/everyone.

Taxes:

Partnership and Multi-Member LLC Taxation:

- **Reporting Income:**

  - The partnership/MMLLC reports its income, deductions, gains, losses, etc., on Form 1065 "U.S. Return of Partnership Income"

  - This form is for informational purposes and does not pay federal taxes directly.

  - This form outlines the partnership's financial activity.

- **K-1 Distribution:**

  - The partnership/MMLLC issues a Schedule K-1 to each partner/member, outlining their share of income, deductions, credits, etc.

  - *Partners/Members use this information for their personal tax returns.*

- **Tax Deadlines:**

  - The tax return (Form 1065) is due on March 15th.

  - The Partnership/MMLLC should also be aware of state-specific tax filing deadlines and comply accordingly.

- **Self-Employment Taxes:**

  - Partners/Members are responsible for paying self-employment taxes (Social Security and Medicare taxes) on their share of the business' income.

    - This typically amounts to 15.3% on top of regular income tax.

  - There are nuances with 'guaranteed pay for services/capital' active partner, passive partner, etc – talk to your accountant for more details.

Tax Deadlines:

- **Form 1065 Due Date:**

  - The filing deadline for Form 1065 is March 15th of each year, or the 15th day of the third month following the end of the Partnership's/MMLLC's tax year.

    - Extensions may be available but require timely filing and specific documentation.

    - If the 1065 goes on extension, keep an eye on if it will be finalized before the 4/15 deadline.

      - If it won't be ready, then you'll need to extend the filing of your Form 1040 as well

        - Don't be terrified of extensions of your tax returns. Not only can they give you more time to fund retirement plans, but they can also allow for a more thorough review of your returns before filing. Being extended doesn't come with any penalty or an increased audit risk. It's not a bad thing to stress about.

- **Schedule K-1 Distribution:** After filing Form 1065, the Partnership/MMLLC provides each partner/member with a Schedule K-1 (Form 1065), which outlines their share of the Partnership's/MMLLC's income, deductions, and credits.

  - Partners/Members use this information to complete their individual tax returns (Form 1040).

- There might also be a requirement to file state returns

  - *We'll talk about income tax nexus and sales tax nexus later.*

Quarterly Tax Obligations:

- Quarterly tax obligations are estimated tax payments made by self-employed individuals, including partnerships, and LLC members, to cover their federal income tax and self-employment tax liabilities.

- **Estimated Payments:**

  - These entities *generally* do not pay federal income tax directly but provide K-1s to Partners/Members.

  - Partners/Members are responsible for estimating and paying quarterly taxes on their share of the entity's income.

- **Payment Frequency:**

  - Federal quarterly tax payments are due four times a year, generally in April, June, September, and January.

    - State estimates may be due on different dates

  - However, the specific due dates may slightly vary each year depending on weekends or holidays.

  - Accurate estimation of these payments helps avoid underpayment penalties.

  - **Pay attention to your state's filing requirements.**

- **IRS Form 1040-ES:**

  - Partners/Members should use Form 1040-ES to calculate estimated tax payments based on their expected income from the partnership/MMLLC.

  - **Using Form 1040-ES:**

    - Remember, the income from your partnership or MMLLC flows through onto your personal income tax return, so the federal estimates you have to make are not via the the entity, but via your own Social Security Number and tax return

    - The IRS provides Form 1040-ES (Estimated Tax for Individuals) to help individuals calculate their quarterly estimated tax payments.

    - The form includes a worksheet to estimate annual income, deductions, and taxes owed, aiding in the determination of quarterly payment amounts.

- **Calculating Quarterly Payments:**

  - These estimated tax payments are each typically about 25% of the individual's projected tax liability for the current tax year (minus any other federal withholding sources)

  - They are calculated based on an estimation of total annual income, deductions, credits, and expected tax liability.

- **Penalties for Underpayments:**

  - Making accurate and timely quarterly payments helps avoid underpayment penalties and interest charges imposed by the IRS.

- If the estimated payments fall short of the actual tax liability, individuals may face penalties for underpayment.

- **A note:** This is not tax advice but I will mention it as I think it fosters good thought, especially for business owners in times of tight cash flow.

  - I've had a lot of very wealthy clients over the years. When they're sending in $50,000 per quarterly, they start to get a little testy. I've heard many of them say that they don't want to give the IRS an "interest-free loan for the year" and that they could make more in their stock market account than they would have to pay in underpayment interest and penalties. *They were willing to pay those for the sake of keeping that money in their metaphorical pockets longer.* Again, I'm not advising you to do so, I'm just pointing out, that as of right now, the IRS is not going to come seize your house, take your first born, kill your dog, and throw you in jail if you don't pay estimates throughout the year.

Tax impact on financial transactions between you and your business:

- **Transaction Tracking with the IRS:**

  - Any money the owners/members put in or take out of the business <u>is</u> a <u>tracked</u> transaction to the IRS

  - (Unlike sole proprietorships or single-member LLCs) For Partnerships and MMLLCs **transactions between the business and its owners or members are meticulously tracked and documented for tax purposes.**

  - Distributions and Contributions:

    - Owners or members can still take distributions or make contributions to the business, but **it's crucial to align these actions with the agreed percentages outlined in the partnership or operating agreement.**

    - For instance, **if partners agree to a 50/50 ownership split, any financial contribution by one partner should be matched by the other to maintain the agreed-upon ownership percentages.**

    - **Adherence to Agreements:** Partnerships and MMLLCs often have specific guidelines in their agreements regarding financial contributions, distributions, and loans. Staying in line with these agreements not only ensures fairness among partners but also maintains the integrity of the ownership structure and tax implications.

- **Loan Transactions:**

  - In these structures, **it's possible to have formal loans between the business and its owners or members.**

    - This includes lending money to the business or borrowing funds from the business.

    - These loan transactions should be properly documented with promissory notes that include terms, interest rates, and repayment schedules to ensure clarity and compliance with IRS regulations.

- **Tax Impact:**

  - These financial transactions may have tax implications for both the business and the individuals involved.

  - Properly documenting loans, contributions, and distributions is <u>essential</u> for accurate tax reporting and compliance.

- It's advisable for partners in a business entity to maintain clear records of all financial transactions, seek legal or accounting advice when necessary, and ensure that actions align with the terms laid out in their partnership or operating agreements.

  - This clarity helps avoid misunderstandings, maintains fair and equitable practices, and ensures compliance with IRS regulations regarding financial dealings within the business entity.

- See Additional Considerations for more details

Common Pitfalls:

- **Wages:**

- You may receive 'guaranteed pay' or a 'partnership/member distribution'

  - Which are treated differently on the return

- As a partner or member, you are NOT a W2 "employee"

- You cannot take a W2 paycheck from your business, but instead can withdraw profits, known as a "distributions," but these distributions aren't considered a business expense or deduction. Guaranteed Pay is a different story – talk to your accountant for more details....

- You still get taxed on the net income of the business, whether you took the money out of the business checking for a 'distribution' or not.

- **Failing to stay in balance to the agreements:**

  - Keep the percentage ownership consistent as you specified in your formal agreements.

    - If you're going to change it up, let your accountant know and amend your partnership or LLC operating agreement

CHAPTER 11

S-Corporation

- An S-Corporation is a distinct legal entity, offering limited liability protection to shareholders while allowing for pass-through taxation.

  ○ Created under "Subchapter S" of the Internal Revenue Code

- **Key Features:**

  ○ **Limited Liability:**

    • Owners are shielded from personal liability related to the company's debts or obligations.

  ○ **Pass-Through Taxation:**

    • Profits and losses "pass through" the corporation to its shareholders' individual tax returns, avoiding double taxation.

  ○ **W-2 Employment:**

    • Shareholders can be W-2 employees, receiving a salary for their services.

- **Pros and Cons:**

  ○ **Pros:**

    • Limited liability, pass-through taxation, and the ability to be a W-2 employee.

  ○ **Cons:**

    • Restrictions on the number and type of shareholders, limitations on the kinds of stock that may be issued, and potential restrictions on foreign ownership.

- **Taxation key points:**

  ○ S-Corps file their tax return (Form 1120S) and the income flows through to the shareholders' personal returns via a K-1 form

- Shareholders can receive distributions/dividends but check with your accountant about the most advantageous tax treatment in your scenario and in your state

- Financial transactions between shareholders and the corporation, including payroll, dividends, and loans, have tax implications. Proper documentation is crucial for compliance and accurate tax reporting.

Steps to Create an S-Corporation

(You'll see that these are all very similar to each other)

- **Choosing a Business Name:**

  - Select a name that aligns with your business vision and ensure it's not already in use by another entity, which you can often determine through your Secretary of State's online business name registry.

  - Check local business registries and domain availability to verify its uniqueness.

- **Registration and Compliance:**

  - File the necessary paperwork with the state to form the corporation.

  - Comply with local regulations, including obtaining licenses or permits required for the corporation's activities.

- **Articles of Incorporation:**

  - File the Articles of Incorporation (to obtain a Certificate of Incorporation) with the Secretary of State or relevant state authority.

  - This legal document establishes the corporation, outlining its purpose, structure, shares authorized to be issued to shareholders, and other essential details

- **Bylaws (these generally do not need to be filed with a state office):**

  - Draft comprehensive bylaws defining internal rules, procedures, and governance frameworks for the corporation's operations.

- Bylaws typically include details on shareholder meetings, director responsibilities, officer roles, voting procedures, and corporate decision-making processes.

- **Tax ID (EIN):**

  - **Obtain an Employer Identification Number (EIN) from the IRS, necessary for tax filings, hiring employees, and other business procedures**

- **Registered Agent:**

  - Appoint a registered agent for legal correspondence from the state, if required.

- **Business Address:**

  - Decide on a business address separate from personal addresses for professional purposes.

  - Options *may* include a physical location, registered agent, PO Box, or virtual business address service.

Bylaws:

Bylaws serve as the backbone of corporate governance and cover various facets, including:

- **Shareholder Meetings:**

  - Outlining procedures for convening and conducting shareholder meetings, specifying notice periods, quorum requirements for meetings, and voting procedures.

- **Board of Directors:**

  - Defining the structure, roles, responsibilities, and powers of the board, including terms, election processes, committees, and decision-making authority.

- **Officer Roles:**

  - Detailing roles and responsibilities of corporate officers (CEO, CFO, etc.), their appointment or election, powers, and obligations.

- **Financial Policies:**

  - Addressing financial matters such as dividends, fiscal year schedules, accounting procedures, and the handling of corporate funds.

- **Amendments and Ratifications:**

  - Establishing protocols for amending bylaws, requiring certain voting thresholds or procedures for revising the articles of incorporation.

- The bylaws serve as an internal guide, ensuring the corporation operates in accordance with predefined rules and regulations, fostering transparency, consistency, and compliance with legal standards. They also demonstrate that the corporation is being operated on a business-like basis and is a distinct entity apart from the personal affairs of the individuals involved, an important factor in preserving the limited personal liability of these individuals.

Taxes:

S-Corporate Taxation:
- **Reporting Income:**

  - The corporation reports its income, deductions, gains, losses, etc., on Form 1120S

    - This results in a Schedule K-1 form that has all of the flow through activity that is then reported on the shareholder's personal return.

    - Remember, your personal 1040 return filing is contingent on the 1120S K-1. You can't file your personal return until the S-corp filing is finished.

- **State Filings:**

  - There might also be a requirement to file state returns

    - *We'll talk about income tax nexus and sales tax nexus later.*

The income that flows through generally will not generate any Self-Employment Taxes, but you will have payroll taxes on your W2 income

Tax Deadlines:
- **Form 1120-S Due Date:**

  - S-Corporations file Form 1120-S by the 15th day of the third month after the end of their tax year.

    - This may be calendar year, or a different fiscal year. Authors will typically be a calendar year but check with your account for that determination in your own scenario.

  - Additionally, adhere to state-specific tax filing deadlines to ensure compliance.

  - Extensions might be available but require prompt filing before the due date with specific documentation.

    - Do not panic if you have to file an extension. There is no 'penalty' for filing an extension, despite what many taxpayers think. There is also no increased audit risk. It's totally fine to need an extension, and in fact, gives you more time to fund any retirement plans. Talk to your advisor for more details.

  - Shareholders receive Schedule K-1 from the S-Corporation, outlining their portion of income or loss, deductions, credits, etc., which they use for their personal tax filings.

- **Quarterly Tax Obligations and Estimated Payments:**

  - Like with the other 'flow-through' entities listed already (Sole-proprietors, SMLLC, Partnerships, MMLLC), the income 'flows though' to the personal tax returns of the 'owners', who are the S-Corp's shareholders.

    - Therefore, federal estimates will be made on the personal returns

  - State return estimates may differ – check with your accountant.

- **Payment Frequency:**

  - Payments are due in April, June, September, and January.

    - State tax estimates may have separate due dates; hence, staying updated on state-specific deadlines is crucial.

- However, the specific due dates may slightly vary each year depending on weekends or holidays.

- They're typically 25% of the estimated tax liability for that year.

- Accurate estimation of these payments helps avoid underpayment penalties.

Tax impact on financial transactions between you and your business:

- **Transaction Tracking with the IRS:**

  - Transactions between the corporation and its shareholders are tracked and documented for tax purposes

    - Distributions to you (the owner/shareholder), are usually:

      - Payroll (wages, bonus)

      - Dividends & distributions

      - Loan to shareholder

        - These loan transactions should be properly documented with promissory notes that include terms, interest rates, and repayment schedules to ensure clarity and compliance with IRS regulations.

    - Putting your money into the corporation, is usually:

      - Loan from shareholder (see notes from loan to shareholder above)

      - Equity transactions: additional stock purchases or capital infusions through Additional Paid in Capital (APIC).

      - Your accountant can help decide which form of funding is most advantageous.

- **Tax Impact:**

  - These financial transactions may have tax implications for both the corporation and shareholders.

- ○ Proper documentation is essential for accurate tax reporting and compliance.

- It's advisable for the shareholders in this business entity to maintain clear records of all financial transactions, seek legal or accounting advice when necessary, and ensure that actions align with the terms laid out in the bylaws.

  - ○ This clarity helps avoid misunderstandings, maintains fair and equitable practices, and ensures compliance with IRS regulations regarding financial dealings within the business entity.

Important Notes / Some Important Pitfalls:

- **Wages:**

  - ○ You DO take a W2 paycheck

  - ○ You are an employee as well as an owner

    - As such, you are now expected to file payroll taxes for your business as well as having payroll taxes withheld from your paycheck

    - Forms 940s, 941s, state payroll tax forms, W3/W2 at year end, etc

      - ○ ADP, QB payroll, etc

- **Risk of Personal Liability:**

  - ○ While shareholders typically have limited liability protection, certain situations, such as piercing the corporate veil due to inadequate corporate governance or co-mingling of personal and business finances, could expose shareholders to personal liability – that's why proper documentation of all transactions between the owner/shareholders and the corporation are so important.

- **Health Insurance**

  - ○ This is a very popular thing that corporate clients often handle incorrectly.

- If your S-Corp pays for your (the officer's) health insurance, please correctly set it up in your system so that it's tracked in your payroll as a taxable benefit (I'm assuming here that the only employees are shareholders (you) and therefore the benefit should not be tax-free). The S-Corp should include the amount of premiums paid on your W2 at year-end. Also, there is usually a footnote on your K-1 that discloses what the amount was. This amount usually flows through onto your Form 1040 as SE health insurance deduction to reduce your taxable income.

- **There's a _very_ popular writer-group rumor that "as soon as you hit $XX,XXX then you should be an S-Corp"**

  - You're going to hate me for saying this but it is VERY state specific, so please consult with a tax professional who knows your state _before_ making a costly tax mistake.

  - If anyone is giving you one-size fits all advice...run.

    - Unless it's me...and I'm telling you to not co-mingle business and personal funds.

      - In that case, it _is_ one-size fits all. Don't cross the streams. **Keep up your money streams entirely separate!**

So, even though the author spheres (and even some very popular people in them) like to circulate that you 'have to' become an S-Corp, or even an LLC, once you hit a certain threshold of income, I'm telling you right now, I **wish** it were that simple. It's 100% not. It's based on so many factors, and you really need to look at your individual state and the needs of you and your business, in connection with getting knowledgeable advice from your tax professional.

- **Am I really paying less in self-employment taxes if I'm an S corp?**

  - It's not that simple.

  - Remember, the government usually gets Social Security and Medicare taxes on W2 wages: 7.65% from the employer, 7.65% from the employee.

  - When you're self-employed and don't have a W2, you're responsible for paying both halves.

  - If you're now an employee of the S-Corp, the corporation is paying its half of the payroll taxes and you as the employee are paying the other half. So.....the 15.3% of taxes is still getting paid (it's just being spread differently and not being paid all on your personal income tax return).

  - There are a couple other differences that I don't really want to get into here, but basically, the S-Corp gets to take the payroll wages and taxes as a deduction on the 1120S return, reducing its taxable income that flows through to you. Just like you would have taken 50% of the SE tax as an adjustment/deduction on your Form 1040 (explained elsewhere)

- Because the S-Corp is a flow-through entity, the ending net income goes onto your (the shareholder's) tax return (Form 1040). That residual income is *not* subject to SE tax, just ordinary income tax, so that's a relief. Remember, you now also have W2 income to report and calculate ordinary income tax on, as well.

- *But this one-size fits all approach needs to go away. I've had millionaire clients operate as Sole Proprietors (and SMLLCs)*

- If you see this "you need to be an S-Corp" advice out there, please know that you *really* should talk with a professional in your area about whether it works for you. There are additional tax considerations that I won't dive into here. But if you can't afford talking with a professional to see whether it's the right choice...*then maybe it's not a good fit*, because it is an entirely separate tax return that I do <u>not</u> advise you to prepare yourself. Remember, any time you create a new entity with its own tax return, you're going to have increased tax prep fees (though of course, those fees are deductible as legitimate business expenses)

- You'll end up doing what you want, but *I do think that if you can't afford an accountant to determine whether it's the right fit, then it might not be the right fit. Don't make a costly tax mistake just because you saw something online (or even here in this book), please confirm with a tax professional who knows <u>your</u> situation.*

CHAPTER 12

C-Corporations

- A C-Corporation (C-Corp) is an independent legal entity distinct from its owners (shareholders) that provides limited liability protection and *has its own tax obligations.*

- **Key Features:**

  - **Limited Liability:**

    - Owners' liability is limited to their investment in the corporation.

  - **Separate Entity:**

    - The corporation is distinct from its shareholders and offers perpetual existence.

  - You can actually be a W2 employee for this entity (unlike for Sole-proprietorships, SMLLC, MMLLC, or Partnerships)

- **Pros and Cons:**

  - **Pros:**

    - Limited liability for shareholders, potential for raising capital through stock sales, and credibility.

  - **Cons:**

    - Double taxation (corporate income taxed at entity level and dividends taxed at the individual level).

    - Possibly the added costs of professional help from attorneys or CPAs for proper setup

- **Important Notes:**

  - **Articles of Incorporation:**

    - File articles of incorporation with the state's Secretary of State and pay associated filing fees.

- **Bylaws:**

  - Establish bylaws outlining the corporation's internal operations, including shareholders' rights and responsibilities.

- **Taxation:**

  - C-Corps file their tax return (Form 1120) and pay corporate income tax on profits.

  - Shareholders are subject to tax on dividends received from the corporation, leading to potential double taxation.

Steps to Create a C-Corporation

(You'll see that these are all very similar to each other)

- **Choosing a Business Name:**

  - Select a name that aligns with your business vision and ensure it's not already in use by another entity.

  - Check local business registries and domain availability to verify its uniqueness.

- **Registration and Compliance:**

  - File the necessary paperwork with the state to register the corporation.

  - Comply with local regulations, including obtaining licenses or permits required for the corporation's activities.

- **Articles of Incorporation:**

  - File the Articles of Incorporation (also known as a Certificate of Incorporation) with the Secretary of State or relevant state authority.

  - This legal document establishes the corporation, outlining its purpose, structure, shares, and other essential details

- **Bylaws:**

- Draft comprehensive bylaws defining internal rules, procedures, and governance frameworks for the corporation's operations.

- Bylaws typically include details on shareholder meetings, director responsibilities, officer roles, voting procedures, and corporate decision-making processes.

- **Tax ID (EIN):**

  - **Obtain an Employer Identification Number (EIN) from the IRS, necessary for tax filings, hiring employees, and other business procedures**

  - Some states may require their own EIN – do your research

- **Registered Agent:**

  - Appoint a registered agent for legal correspondence, if applicable

- **Business Address:**

  - Decide on a business address separate from personal addresses for professional purposes.

  - Options include a physical location, PO Box, or virtual business address service.

Bylaws:

Bylaws serve as the backbone of corporate governance and cover various facets, including:
- **Shareholder Meetings:**

  - Outlining procedures for convening and conducting shareholder meetings, specifying notice periods, quorum requirements, and voting procedures.

- **Board of Directors:**

  - Defining the structure, roles, responsibilities, and powers of the board, including terms, election processes, committees, and decision-making authority.

- **Officer Roles:**

  - Detailing roles and responsibilities of corporate officers (CEO, CFO, etc.), their appointment, powers, and obligations.

- **Financial Policies:**

  - Addressing financial matters such as dividends, fiscal year schedules, accounting procedures, and the handling of corporate funds.

- **Amendments and Ratifications:**

  - Establishing protocols for amending bylaws, requiring certain voting thresholds or procedures for changes.

The bylaws serve as an internal guide, ensuring the corporation operates in accordance with predefined rules and regulations, fostering transparency, consistency, and compliance with legal standards

Please research "piercing the corporate veil" —> you don't want to do this. If you're going to create a business, keep the business activity separate from your personal activity.

Issuing Stock – Information Your Accountant Wants

I cannot stress this enough. This is not legal advice.

- Issuing stock requires careful consideration of legal and financial implications.

- It's often best to consult legal counsel or financial advisors to ensure adherence to relevant laws and best practices throughout the issuance process.

- As a CPA, I *never* helped a client prepare the issuance of stock, that was always left to the attorney.

  - What *is* relevant to your return is the number of shares issued, if its common or preferred stock, the number of shares bought back, and the valuation of that stock.

- Always tell your accountant if you did anything with the stock during the year (issued more, bought back, gifted any, etc)

Taxes:

C-Corporate Taxation:

- **Reporting Income:**

  - The corporation reports its income, deductions, gains, losses, etc., on Form 1120

  - This form outlines the corporation's financial activity.

  - There is no K-1 or flow through income onto your personal return.

- **State Filings:**

  - There might also be a requirement to file state returns

    - *We'll talk about income tax nexus and sales tax nexus later.*

You won't have any Self-Employment Taxes, but you probably will have payroll taxes now

Tax Deadlines:

- **Form 1120 Due Date:**

  - File Form 1120 by the corporation's tax year's 15th day of the fourth month after its year-end

    - It's worded funky because some businesses don't operate on a calendar year.

  - Corporations should also be aware of state-specific tax filing deadlines and comply accordingly.

  - Extensions may be available but require timely filing and specific documentation.

  - Unlike some of the other entities, an extension of an 1120 Corporate return, does not affect your personal 1040 filing.

    - Instead, the only thing from the corporation that you need to file your personal income tax return is your W2 (and potentially any dividends, distributions, or interest)

○ Of course, there would also be reporting if you were to sell any stock.

Quarterly Tax Obligations:

- Quarterly tax obligations include estimated tax payments made by C-Corps to cover federal income tax liabilities

- **Estimated Payments:**

  ○ C-Corps are responsible for paying estimated taxes based on their anticipated annual income, deductions, and tax liability.

  ○ Payments should be about 25% of the projected annual tax liability divided into quarterly installments.

- **Payment Frequency:**

  ○ Federal quarterly tax payments are typically due in April, June, September, and December.

    - State tax estimates may have separate due dates; hence, staying updated on state-specific deadlines is crucial.

    - However, the specific due dates may slightly vary each year depending on weekends or holidays.

  ○ Accurate estimation of these payments helps avoid underpayment penalties.

- **IRS Form 1120-W:**

  ○ Use Form 1120-W to calculate estimated tax payments based on projected annual income, deductions, and taxes owed.

  ○ Accurate estimation helps avoid underpayment penalties.

Tax impact on financial transactions between you and your business:

- **Transaction Tracking with the IRS:**

  - Transactions between the corporation and its shareholders are tracked and documented for tax purposes in C-Corps.

    - Distributions to you (the owner/shareholder), are usually:

      - Payroll (wages, bonus)

      - Dividends

      - Loan to shareholder

        - Formal loans between the corporation and shareholders are possible, requiring proper documentation with terms, interest rates, and repayment schedules.

    - Putting your money into the corporation, is usually:

      - Loan from shareholder (see notes from loan to shareholder above)

      - Equity transactions: Additional stock purchases, capital infusions via Additional Paid in Capital (APIC)

- **Tax Impact:**

  - These financial transactions may have tax implications for both the corporation and shareholders.

  - Proper documentation is essential for accurate tax reporting and compliance.

- It's advisable for the shareholders of this business entity to maintain clear records of all financial transactions, seek legal or accounting advice when necessary, and ensure that actions align with the terms laid out in the bylaws.

  - This clarity helps avoid misunderstandings, maintains fair and equitable practices, and ensures compliance with IRS regulations regarding financial dealings within the business entity.

Important Notes / Some Important Pitfalls:

- **Wages:**

  - You DO take a W2 paycheck

  - You are an employee

    - As such, you are now expected to file payroll taxes for your business as well as having payroll taxes withheld from your paycheck

    - Forms 940s, 941s, state payroll tax forms, W3/W2 at year end, etc

      - ADP, QB payroll, etc

- **Double Taxation:**

  - Shareholders of C-corps are at risk of double taxation

    - Once from the corporate taxes on the net income of the corporation (paid for and by the corporate entity itself on it's own tax return) but also again at the shareholder individual level due to personal income taxes on any dividends and other distributions paid.

  - This *can* lead to higher overall tax liabilities.

  - **Loss of Pass-Through Taxation:**

    - Unlike S Corporations and other pass-through entities, C Corporations don't offer pass-through taxation.

    - Income is taxed at the corporate level before distribution to shareholders, potentially resulting in higher tax liabilities.

- **Complexity and Compliance:**

  - C Corporations typically have more extensive compliance requirements, including regular filings, record-keeping, and administrative duties.

  - Failure to comply can result in penalties or legal issues.

- **Stockholder Disputes:**

  - With multiple shareholders, conflicts may arise concerning decision-making, dividends, or corporate direction.

- ○ Clear governance structures and agreements are essential to navigate potential disputes.

- ○ Maybe not so relevant here in the writerly world, but as your business scales, who knows.

- **Higher Formation and Ongoing Costs:**

  - ○ Setting up and maintaining a C Corporation can be more expensive due to legal and administrative requirements, including fees for filing, compliance, and ongoing operational costs.

- **Risk of Personal Liability:**

  - ○ While shareholders typically have limited liability protection, certain situations, such as *piercing the corporate veil* due to inadequate corporate governance or co-mingling of personal and business finances, could expose shareholders to personal liability

CHAPTER 13
Due Dates for 2024 federal estimates for calendar year taxpayers:

1st payment ....April 15, 2024

2nd payment ....June 17, 2024

3rd payment ....Sept. 16, 2024

4th payment ....Jan. 15, <u>2025</u>

CHAPTER 14

Additional Considerations

These are pretty standard unless otherwise noted. As always, consult with your own legal counsel or accountant for applicability but maybe these items will prompt a conversation

- **Registered Agent:**

  - Depending on the state, appoint a registered agent who acts as the official contact for legal correspondence on behalf of the business entity.

- **EINs**

  - Federal Employer Identification Number (EIN)

  - It's like a Social Security Number for your business entity

  - It is FREE from the IRS – if someone is trying to sell you one...run.

  - You can go directly to the IRS website and apply. You just need to choose your entity type and you'll get your number within a few minutes

  - Some states require State EINs as well. Check your specific regulations

- **Annual Filings and Compliance:**

  - Understand and fulfill any annual reporting requirements, fees, or renewals stipulated by your state or local government for continued business operation.

- **Legal Compliance:**

  - Adhere to legal and regulatory requirements.

  - Maintain separate business accounts and meticulous records.

- **Business Address:**

  - *Sole Proprietorship*: Consider setting up a business address separate from your home address for a professional image.

- Options include using a PO Box or obtaining a virtual business address service.

  - *Single-Member LLC*: An SMLLC typically requires a registered office address for legal and official correspondence, which can be a physical address or a registered agent's address.

    - Same with partnerships, MMLLCs, and Corporations (C and S)

- **Licenses and Permits:**

  - Research and obtain any necessary business licenses or permits required for your industry or locality.

  - This may include state or local permits, professional licenses, or specific industry-related certifications.

  - Some states require a business license

  - Check into sales tax requirements, if necessary, or if you need any Resale Certificates or Seller's Permits

    - We have a section on sales tax elsewhere

- **Business Insurance:**

  - Evaluate the need for business insurance to protect against unforeseen risks or liabilities.

  - Consider general liability insurance, professional liability (errors and omissions) insurance, or business property insurance based on your business needs.

- **Accounting System:**

  - Implement an accounting system to track income, expenses, and taxes *accurately* and *consistently*

  - These systems streamline financial processes, ensuring meticulous record-keeping and facilitating easier tax preparation and reporting.

    - It's not just about having a system but consistently using it to maintain accurate financial records.

  - Consider using accounting software or hiring an accountant to set up a robust system tailored to your business.

  - *This book has an entire section devoted to this*

- **Professional Services:**

  - Consider engaging legal and financial professionals, such as attorneys or accountants, for guidance on legal structures, compliance, tax optimization, and ongoing financial management.

  - Tax Prep:

    - While you might be able to prep your own Schedule C return (sole-proprietor or Single-member LLC), it's not like you will be able to do your own 1065: Partnership or MMLLC, 1120 C-Corp return, or 1120S S-Corp return. Anticipate those tax prep costs. My firm wouldn't even touch a business return for less than $2,000 in fees. Your area of the world, and preparer, might have a different threshhold, but there is a lot that goes into them.

    - Also, with the advent of K-2 and K-3s on the 1065 and 1120S tax returns, things because a bit more complicated and time-consuming. If you see your return grow a lot thicker than it used to be, blame the foreign income reporting requirements that now require your preparer to allocate your income by source country and report any associated foreign taxes and expenses

- **Website and Online Presence:**

  - Possibly establish an online presence through a website or social media platforms to market your business and interact with customers.

  - Ensure compliance with any legal requirements for online business activities.

    - For example, on your website, some countries require terms of service, privacy policies, etc. Also, email newsletters need to have certain verbiage and disclosures in some countries. Do your research.

  - If writing under a pen name – search the internet for it first. Make sure you won't be competing with an internet sensation for search engine hits when fans of yours try to look you up.

- **Operational Organization Tips:**

  - Develop a systematic approach to manage administrative tasks, track expenses, and maintain records effectively.

  - Use a calendar or task management system to stay organized with deadlines, tax filings, and important business events.

  - Regularly review and update your business infrastructure to adapt to changing needs and comply with evolving legal or regulatory requirements.

- **Money**

  - *<u>Keep your personal finances separate from the business finances</u>*

  - <u>**Set up a separate checking account, credit card, email account (can be a free outlook account where receipts will be emailed and stored), PayPal/Venmo/CashApp, etc.**</u> While you're at it, you can also create an Amazon KDP, IngramSpark, Bowker, Canva, stock photo sites, UPS/Fedex, etc with that email.

    - There are a number of good reasons why you should do this, but one tangible one is for bookkeeping purposes

      - Do you want to comb through your personal bank account every year and have to remember which transactions were for your business and which were for your household? No.

      - Do yourself a favor, get those items separated right from the start and save yourself (or your accountant) a lot of headache.

        - Coming from a CPA – PLEASE :-)

  - Avoiding the commingling of funds is vital to maintain the legal separation between personal and business finances. Combining these funds can jeopardize limited liability protection and complicate accounting processes.

  - **For Partnerships/MMLLCs:**

    - Maintain a clear separation between personal and business finances by **establishing distinct accounts for each partner/member.**

      - When I set up a client's QuickBooks or do tax prep: I make it so each Partner/Member has their own Equity account, Contributions account, and Distributions account. I do the same for all of the other Partners/Members as well.

        - The money they put in goes into Contributions, the money they take out goes through Distributions, and their capital account goes to Equity.

        - At the end of tax prep, all of those number tie perfectly to the tax return numbers.

      - This segregation eases bookkeeping and protects against legal issues by preserving the separation between personal and business assets.

      - For MMLLCs in particular, preserving the distinctness of personal and business finances is essential to uphold limited liability protection and streamline accounting processes.

- Avoiding commingling funds is crucial to prevent legal complications and complexities.

- **Missing Tax Deadlines**:

  - Stay updated on tax filing deadlines, including quarterly estimated tax payments, to avoid penalties for late or underpayment.

    - Don't forget any state income taxes, sales taxes, payroll taxes, VAT, etc

  - For the flow-through entities (sole-proprietorship, SMLLC, MMLLC, partnership, and S-crop), remember, the federal quarterly tax payments are made via your own tax return forms.

  - For C-corps, the quarterly estimates are made on behalf of the corporation

- **Failure to File 1099-MISC**:

  - Ensure compliance with IRS regulations by filing Form 1099-MISC/NEC for payments over $600 made to subcontractors or vendors, unless specific exceptions apply.

  - However, exemptions exist if payments were made through certain platforms like PayPal business or if the subcontractor themselves is a C-Corp or S-Corp.

  - Note: LLC stands for Limited Liability *Company*, not Limited Liability *Corporation*. If they have "LLC" in their business name, be safe and ask them for a W9. If they check the box as being anything other than a C or S Corp → 1099 them (again, if you paid them over $600 and it wasn't for supplies)

  - The penalties for not complying are big. Don't skip this if necessary

  - *This book has an entire section devoted to this*

  - If *you* are an S or C corp, you still have to issue these to others when applicable

  - Filing thresholds

    - $10 or more in royalties and they need to receive a 1099

    - $600 or more in services and they need to receive a 1099

  - Different rules apply for 1099s if your subcontractor is foreign – look on the IRS's site for the most up-to-date information.

CHAPTER 15

*Limited Liability (to an extent)

In some instances, you might have noticed my mention of "limited liability *(to an extent)*."

It's crucial to clarify that while this information is not legal advice, authors often encounter legal exposure primarily in areas such as defamation, privacy, or infringement claims.

These legal challenges typically arise due to an author's *personal* actions rather than the business's, making liability a personal matter regardless of whether one operates under an LLC or Inc. designation.

One effective way to protect oneself, irrespective of being an LLC or corporation, is through insurance coverage.

Analyze your situation and figure out what is best for you.

CHAPTER 16

Choosing Pen Names, DBAs, and Company Names

Pen Name:
- A pen name, also known as a pseudonym, is a fictitious name used by an author instead of their real name.

- Authors often adopt pen names for various reasons, including privacy concerns, genre differentiation, or to create a distinctive authorial identity.

- Researching the chosen pen name across search engines and book databases is essential to ensure it's unique and not already associated with another author's work.

- When publishing under a pen name, remember to look at the differing copyright terms/lengths

- Some states require pen names to be registered as trade names – check your secretary of state

DBA (Doing Business As)
- A DBA, or "Doing Business As," is a *registered* trade name under which a business operates that differs from its legal entity's name.

- It allows individuals or entities to conduct business under a name that is not their legal name.

- However, a DBA does not provide legal protection or establish a separate legal entity.

- It's important to verify the uniqueness of the chosen DBA by checking federal, state (and sometimes regional) business registries and databases to avoid conflicts with existing businesses operating under similar names.

- Consult with an attorney about filing a Fictitious Business Name Statement – it may be required where you live

Company Name Considerations:
- When establishing a legal entity such as an LLC (Limited Liability Company), corporation, or any formal business structure, the chosen name must comply with specific legal requirements.

- For instance:

  - If you're forming an LLC, the chosen name typically ends with "LLC" or its full form, "Limited Liability Company."

    - Ensure the name's uniqueness by searching state business registries and databases to avoid conflicts.

  - For corporations, names often contain terms like "Inc.," "Corp.," or "Corporation."

    - Similar to an LLC, verify the availability and uniqueness of the chosen name through state business databases and trademark searches.

  - Alternatively, you CANNOT use these initials if your entity is NOT what you're using the abbreviation for

    - If you aren't forming an LLC, you cannot use 'LLC' at the end

    - If you aren't forming a corporation, you cannot use "Inc." at the end

Trademark Searches:

- Conducting thorough trademark searches is crucial before finalizing any name, be it a pen name, DBA, or company name.

- This helps ensure that the chosen name is not already trademarked or in use by another entity, preventing potential legal issues or infringement claims in the future.

- Utilize trademark databases and consult legal counsel if needed to secure the chosen name and protect your intellectual property rights.

CHAPTER 17

The Balance Sheet

A balance sheet is a financial statement that provides a snapshot of a company's financial position at a specific point in time.

It presents a summary of what a company owns (assets), what it owes (liabilities), and the shareholders' equity.

Here's a breakdown:
- **Assets**: These are the resources owned by the company, including tangible items like cash, inventory, equipment, and property, as well as intangible assets such as copyrights, patents, or trademarks.

- **Liabilities**: These represent the company's obligations or debts, including loans, accounts payable, credit card liabilities, accrued expense like payroll liabilities, and other financial responsibilities.

- **Shareholders' Equity**: This section reflects the ownership interest in the company.

  ○ It's calculated as assets minus liabilities and includes common stock, retained earnings, and additional paid-in capital.

The balance sheet follows the equation:
Assets = Liabilities + Shareholders' Equity
This equation ensures that the company's resources (assets) are financed by either borrowing money (liabilities) or through the contributions of the shareholders (equity).

The balance sheet provides insight into a company's solvency, liquidity, and overall financial health.

If your *balance* sheet doesn't *balance*...you have some problems.

You don't report your balance sheet information when filing a Federal Schedule C tax return, but you do need to include a balance sheet on all other federal returns (1065: Partnership, Multi-Member LLC, 1120 C-Corp, or 1120S S-Corp). Check your state for their specific filing requirements.

Chapter 18

The Income Statement (Profit & Loss)

An income statement, also known as a profit and loss statement (P&L), is a financial statement that summarizes a company's revenues, expenses, gains, and losses over a specific period.

It gives a comprehensive view of a company's financial performance.

Comparing it year over year can be incredibly useful for a variety of reasons: consistency in reporting, growth or lagging, mis-posted items, etc.

Here's what it typically includes:

- Revenue:

  - Gross receipts of income for a business

  - This section shows the total amount of money earned from the sale of goods or services.

  - It's often broken down by different sources or categories of sales.

- Cost of Goods Sold (COGS):

  - This represents the direct costs associated with producing the goods or services sold.

  - It includes expenses like raw materials, labor, and manufacturing overhead.

  - Some authors put the book production costs here but I don't

- Gross Profit

  - Calculated as Revenue minus COGS, it reflects the profit generated after deducting the direct costs of producing goods or services.

- Operating Expenses:

  - These are the costs incurred from running the day-to-day operations of the business, such as salaries, rent, utilities, marketing, and administrative expenses.

- Operating Income (or Loss):

  - Calculated by subtracting operating expenses from the gross profit, it indicates the profit (or loss) generated from the core operations of the business.

- Other Income and Expenses:

  - This section includes gains or losses from non-operational activities, such as interest income, investments, or one-time events like the sale of assets.

- **<u>Net</u> Income (or Net Loss):**

  - This is the final figure and represents the company's overall profitability.

  - "The bottom line"

  - "In the black" = profitable

  - "In the red" = at a loss

  - It's calculated by subtracting total expenses (including operating expenses and other income/expenses) from the gross profit.

    - Net Income/loss = All revenue minus all expenses

The income statement is crucial for assessing a company's ability to generate profit, manage expenses, and achieve operational efficiency over a specific period, usually quarterly or annually.

It provides valuable insights into the company's financial performance and profitability.

**A note – you may hear/read people talking about their 'income' for the year. It can be hard to tell whether they are talking about their 'gross receipts,' (their total revenue received/earned) or if they are talking about their *net* income (their bottom line).

CHAPTER 19

Budgeting

I think the current statistic is that most self-employed businesses go belly up within the first **five** years.

The biggest problem? Cash Flow.

"Being an author doesn't seem like a big cash outlay, isn't it just putting your ideas down in a manuscript and selling it?" (cue all of us authors grinding our teeth as we think about what we've spent on editors, covers, marketing, formatting, and more)

Budgeting is a critical aspect of managing any business, and for authors, it's no different.

Anticipating your annual expenses and planning for them are crucial steps in sustaining your business. Consider the range of costs involved: from mundane essentials like PO Boxes and software subscriptions to substantial investments in marketing, website maintenance, editing tools, and memberships. These are your backbone expenses, the ones you know are on the horizon, waiting to be dealt with.

It's essential to run the numbers, create a projection of your yearly expenses, and use that as a guide to steer your financial decisions. Knowing what's coming and having a realistic view of your financial obligations allows you to plan wisely. For instance, if your budget shows tight cash flow in December, it might not be the best time to hire an editor or make substantial investments. Instead, strategize to stagger your expenses, perhaps delaying certain costs until a more financially stable period. Or, alternatively, if you're trying to drive down your taxable income, maybe you do want to pay your editor before December is over, even if you aren't scheduled to pay until January (if you're cash basis).

However, it doesn't stop there. Budgeting isn't just about managing expenses; it's also about strategizing income generation. Once you've estimated your spend, the next step is to devise plans to secure the income necessary to cover those expenses.

This strategic approach to budgeting ensures not only that you're aware of your financial commitments but also that you're proactively aligning your efforts to meet these obligations. It's a balance between managing your expenses and steering your income-generating activities toward fulfilling those financial needs.

By practicing prudent budgeting, especially in the formative years of your business, you're setting a foundation for financial stability. It's about making informed decisions, strategizing your financial moves, and positioning yourself for sustained success in the competitive world of authorship.

- Some examples of predictable yearly expenses

- PO Boxes

- Microsoft (Word, PowerPoint, Excel)

- Monthly advertising spend

- Website

- Any editing software programs

- Canva / other graphics

- Book Funnel / Story Origin

- Book Sirens / Book Sprout

- Any membership dues

- LLC or state registrations

- ISBNs, Copyrights

- Editors / beta readers

- World Anvil / Trello / Notion / etc

- Etc

The best part? Most of these expenses are the same amount, or close to it, year over year. That makes budgeting a breeze.

Figure out your fixed costs and work backwards – there's your minimum target for revenue in order to break even! Now, get writing!

I apologize for all the words in this segment. I couldn't find a way to create bite-sized chunks. Hopefully, I didn't put you to sleep!

CHAPTER 20

Royalties

As an author, the royalties you earn from platforms like Amazon, IngramSpark, Draft2Digital (D2D), wide distributors, direct sales, and others are a significant part of your income.

It's crucial to comprehend how to report these earnings accurately

- **Royalty Reporting:**

    - Report royalties from platforms (Amazon, IngramSpark, D2D) on your designated entity (Schedule C, 1065, 1120, 1120S).

    - Base your reported income on what you were **paid** in the tax year, not solely on what you've earned.

        - See cash vs. accrual section for more details

    - Verify amounts using bank statement deposits for accuracy.

        - Sometimes 1099s can be incorrect – we all make mistakes – even the 'Zon

- **Payment Timing:**

    - Note the 60-day delay in receiving payments from these platforms.

    - Income earned in December 2023, for instance, may not be received until 2024.

        - If that's the case, it doesn't go on your 2023 tax return

            - Unless you're accrual basis

    - Authors typically operate on a cash basis.

        - Report income when received, aligning with actual payment receipt.

- **International Earnings:**

- Royalty payments from Amazon, etc usually don't create tax obligations in other countries.

- Such earnings typically don't establish a tax presence (nexus) in those regions.

- For instance, Amazon is a distributor and collects and remits those taxes themselves. They just pay you what's left over after they take their cut. They're the entity selling in those countries (or even states, for that matter), not you yourself.

  - But direct sales...

- **Direct Sales Consideration:**

  - Different rules apply to direct sales

  - Specific details on managing direct sales and their tax implications will be covered separately.

CHAPTER 21

The Crucial Role of Record-Keeping and Organization

I can't stress enough how important a good record-keeping system is. It's right up there with keeping your business finances separate from your personal finances.

Why Records Matter:

- In case the IRS ever comes knocking...Imagine your finances as a reliable assistant, documenting every transaction, expense, and income source.

- **HOT TIP:** Whenever you send money to a governmental agency (IRS or state department of revenue) MAKE A COPY OF THE CHECK before you mail it. (Or you can pay on their IRS Direct Pay website electronically)

  - Second part – mail it Certified Mail Receipt.

  - Store the copies together in your records.

- My experience: I have had *many* calls with the IRS over the years where the client made a federal estimate to the IRS, and the IRS said they never received it. It then requires the client to go to the bank, get a copy of the cancelled check (front and back), call the IRS back, be on hold for three hours, and then they track the code on the back of the check. SEVERAL times, the IRS received the check and then deposited it to the wrong taxpayer's account. 100% true story. This has not just happened once.

  - For the people who don't like paper checks, the IRS has a Direct Pay option on their .gov website. You can pay taxes and estimates there as well. Save the confirmation page as a pdf. Store it. You might need it someday.

- Any images used on your cover? Keep copies of those licenses for as long as your book is published. You never know when the bots will come knocking and demand a copy of your licenses.

  - This has happened to me too! Nothing like begging all your cover designers for copies of licenses for the images and fonts used and hoping you can get them submitted before your account is suspended...

- Make sure you also keep copies of your home office expenses if you choose to claim them on your taxes.

- The common rule of thumb is to keep most records/receipts/invoices/etc for seven years, tax returns forever, and any contracts/licenses for as long as the work is out on the market.

- The statute of limitations on auditing tax returns refers to the time limit the Internal Revenue Service (IRS) has to examine or audit your tax return. Once this period expires, the IRS generally cannot pursue additional assessments or adjustments related to that specific tax year.

  - The general statute of limitations for auditing a tax return is three years from the date you filed it or the due date of the return, whichever is later.

  - Generally, if you substantially underreport your income (by 25% or more), the IRS has six years to initiate an audit.

  - If the IRS suspects fraud or if you never file a tax return, there is no statute of limitations. In such cases, they can audit your return **at any time**.

  - If you file an amended tax return, the statute of limitations is generally three years from the date of the amended return or within two years from the time you paid the tax, whichever is later.

  - State tax authorities may have their own statutes of limitations, which can vary

- You can see how keeping records for more than just one year can be important, yes?

Time is Money:

- People, like anyone else, value time. Sorting through a chaotic pile of receipts or folders is time wasted. Organized records mean quick access to financial data, saving you time for what matters most – your author business

- Disorganized finances lead to confusion. It's not just about finding receipts; it's about understanding where your money goes, gauging spending patterns, and making informed decisions. Organized finances offer clarity and control.

Efficient Planning:

- Planning doesn't have to be overwhelming. With organized records, financial management becomes straightforward. No more last-minute rushes – just a well-prepared script that minimizes stress and maximizes financial stability.

- Your financial story is about thriving, not just surviving. Organized records empower you to make informed decisions. Know your expenses, grasp your income, and plan a course that aligns with your financial goals.

Tools for Organization:
- Explore digital tools that make record-keeping hassle-free. From budgeting apps to cloud-based storage, technology offers practical solutions.

- I have a variety of offerings (currently):

    ○ I have a physical journal that you can purchase if you're a paper-records kind of person.

    ○ I have simple, and more customized Excel trackers, if you like Excel

    ○ I have lessons on how to set up a QuickBooks Online (QBO) account to do a lot of the work for you

    ○ I also offer customized QBO set-ups for you

How much is your time worth? You might not think that keeping track of your expenses every month is important.

When asked about your bookkeeping do you answer, "what bookkeeping? [and shrug it off with a laugh]?"

- Is your time worth more than:

    ○ Northeast: $200 to $400 per hour

    ○ West Coast: $150 and $300 per hour

    ○ Midwest: $100 and $250 per hour

    ○ South: $100 and $250 per hour

- Or, if you have a bookkeeper:

    ○ Northeast: $40 to $100 per hour

- West Coast: $35 and $85 per hour

- Midwest: $30 and $70 per hour

- South: $30 and $65 per hour

Think of that the next time you leave your receipts in a shoe box and ask your CPA to run a subtotal of everything for you.

You could save yourself so much money and stress if you just put systems in place to do it for you. If you're willing to pay an accountant to do that for you every year, that's totally fine.

If you want to scramble every February to try to compile everything for the prior year for your tax return, that's fine too.

But how are you tracking your success?

How are you finding out whether or not a series is profitable or whether or not a certain pen name is dragging your income down year after year?

A proper record-keeping system can help with that

Receipts - what do you do with them?

- Electronic copies are great! Make sure to back them up somewhere just in case. You don't want to get audited two years from now and have nothing to show the auditor (they don't like that).

  - This is when keeping those personal funds separate from the business funds is so awesome.

  - Go to PayPal and save the PDF of the year's activity. Boom, done. Go to Square, print the year's activity. Done again. No need to go through and cross of personal items.

- Paper copies of backups are also fine, but just try to have a system

  - Do you want to organize by date? By type of expense? By vendor?

  - Just try to figure out a system that makes sense (and that you'll remember and be consistent with. Try not to put website expenses under advertising and then put more website expenses under office expense. It's not the end of the world if you mess it up, but do your best.)

  - There are programs that allow you to take a picture of your paper receipts and will convert them into PDFs for you. Or you can just go the old-fashioned way and scan them on your scanner or printer :-)

CHAPTER 22

Expenses vs. Asset

- **Expense:**

  - Expenses are immediate costs incurred in running your business operations.

  - They are typically items or services that are consumed or used up quickly within the current accounting period.

  - Expenses are deducted from the revenue in the year they are paid, reducing taxable income for that year.

    - Paid if cash basis, incurred if accrual

  - Examples: Office supplies, utilities, rent, salaries, advertising costs, and other day-to-day operational expenses fall under this category.

- **Asset:**

  - Assets are items of value that provide future benefits to the business and are expected to be used over a longer period.

  - They are initially recorded as assets on the balance sheet and are typically not fully expensed in the year of purchase.

    - Current depreciation laws actually are allowing the full cost of the asset to be depreciated in most instances depending on the asset. It still needs to go through the balance sheet first though. Check with your accountant

  - Assets are subject to depreciation or amortization, where their costs are spread over their useful life, reflecting their gradual loss of value.

  - Examples: Property, equipment, vehicles, patents, trademarks, and other long-term investments are classified as assets and are typically capitalized and depreciated over time.

- **Policy Adherence:**

  - Establish and maintain consistent policies within your business operations. This includes financial management, expense reporting, and asset handling.

  - Consistent policies streamline bookkeeping, making it more efficient and less prone to errors.

- **De Minimis Safe Harbor IRS Rule:**

  - The IRS has a de minimis safe harbor election allowing the immediate expensing of certain low-value assets.

  - For instance, if an equipment or furniture purchase is below a specific cost threshold (such as $2,500), you can expense it in the year of purchase rather than depreciating it over time.

  - Assets falling under this threshold can be treated as expenses, reducing the administrative burden of depreciation.

  - Anything less than $2,500 can be put in an expense bucket, anything over, put to an asset, *and then* check with your accountant.

  - It's an election on your tax return – look for something called **Section 1.263** – it's 'elected' fresh every year

- **Detailed Documentation:**

  - Keeping detailed memos, receipts, and documentation for all purchases and financial transactions is crucial.

  - Comprehensive records not only assist in accurate tax preparation but also save time for your tax preparer, potentially reducing accounting costs.

We'll break down the various expense buckets elsewhere

CHAPTER 23

What does your tax preparer want at tax time?

"They don't want your receipts. They don't want your receipts. They don't want your receipts."

Ok, now that we know that your preparer doesn't want your receipts, what do they want? Ideally? Probably for you to run the subtotals for them and then they'll ask for follow-up information later as needed.

Some items they may request (though it really varies on the preparer and the actual entity type and activity level):

- Financial Reports

  - Income statement (also called a Profit and Loss)

  - Balance sheet (you'll want to make sure the balances are accurate, i.e – credit card balance at year-end, loan balances at year-end, bank balance at year-end, etc)

  - General ledger (a listing of all of your transactions over the course of the year) (*sometimes*)

    - They would use this to scan for dating/categorization issues

    - They will also scan for large items that may need to be capitalized (equipment over $2,500)

      - THAT is when they may want a receipt

      - If they see an invoice that you paid for $3,500, they'll want to see what it was for (providing your details aren't clear).

      - This is because if you paid $3,500 to Apple for instance, $3,000 of that might be for a computer, and $500 might be for small supplies/accessories.

        - That transaction above is reported differently than if you bought: 1 macbook, 2 ipads, and some small accessories.

          - That's when your invoice backup is important

- Of course, if you use an online accounting system like QBO (Quickbooks Online), your life just got a whole lot easier.

  - You can just give them accountant's log in access, they can log in, pull all the reports themselves, and just ask you questions when necessary.

  - You'll save time, stress, money if your finances are clean and tidy

- Other things they'll probably ask for:

  - Were you required to file 1099's? If so, did you?

  - Total mileage and total business mileage (they need both)

  - Any home office deduction information (discussed more elsewhere)

  - Any sales in other states / countries? If so, where?

  - Any retirement contributions made / do you want to make any?

  - Any federal/state estimated tax payments made? If so, when?

  - Did you reconcile your bank statements?

  - Did you remember to include the expenses that were on your credit card at 12/31 but you hadn't paid off yet?

I have a check list that your preparer will ask for on my website. Take a look. It's free and you can use it to prep your information for tax season

CHAPTER 24

Accounting tools

In the digital age, managing your finances is no longer confined to dusty ledgers and manual calculations. There is a diverse range of accounting tools that can transform your financial burden.

You can find more from an internet search but I'll drop some ideas/names below for you to research further:

- Paper log books / journals

    - *I created one for authors, and even though it's brilliant, I'm not a 'paper tracker' kind of person. If you are though, it's available for sale*

- Excel / Sheets / Etc (any spreadsheet software)

    - This requires more manual input but can still be a powerful tool, especially with it's free nature

    - Usually can be set up so it can be accessed and updated from anywhere via OneDrive, Google, etc.

    - Can run subtotals and do the 'math' for you – less operator error

    - *I have an incredible one that I designed that is fool-proof. It can track over multiple years of income and expenses, track mileage, and home office expenses too. It even creates a draft version of your Schedule C tax return automatically.*

        - *It's also available for sale online.*

- **QuickBooks Online and Desktop:**

    - Personally, I use QBO (QuickBooks Online) for my business and I LOVE it.

    - If you link your bank feeds (and credit card feeds and PayPal even), it can learn what various repeat expenses are for. You can actually set up 'rules' so that anytime something is charged to Staples, it goes to 'Office Expense' – that sort of thing. I love the automation of it all because even though I love accounting, I love automated efficiency more :-)

- There is a monthly fee for QBO that can be prohibitive for many, but when you figure out what your time is worth as your author business grows, I find the cost well worth the time-saving.

- *I have a series of videos exploring exactly how you can use it to take charge of your finances and how it can totally transform your business strategy (but any online platform would work, I just have experience in QBO)*

- FreshBooks

- Wave

- Zoho Books

- Xero

- Xpense

- Quicken

- Tiller

- Etc.

CHAPTER 25

Accounting best practices for authors who use software for tracking

If your accountant prepares journal entries for your QuickBooks (etc) file in the course of their tax prep, *please* post those adjustments in your own file. This will make your financials tie to the tax return.

Hot tip: once you've sent your information to your tax preparer, do not post any more transactions to the year that the preparer is working on. <u>It will mess things up</u>. If you sent them the file to prepare taxes for Year 20**XX**, do not post any more transactions dated with 20**XX**. Post those to 20**XY**, unless you've discussed with your accountant and they know what you are doing.

Pro tip: if you're a 1065 or 1120/1120S filer, and your capital section of your accounting file doesn't tie to your prior year's tax return, your accountant has to match up every single beginning balance sheet item on your records to the records on your PY return. If they don't match, we have to make adjustments to tie them out. Time = money. Make them match — Post the entries and don't mess with the year that your accountant is working on.

Your wallet and your mentally drained CPA will thank you

CHAPTER 26

Authorpreneurship

In the ever-evolving landscape of authorship, creating diverse income streams is a great strategy for financial stability.

Let's explore a range of avenues beyond traditional book sales that can contribute to your author income portfolio. This is not an exhaustive list (nor am I offering recommendations) and it's always changing but here are some basic streams:

Paperbacks and Hardbacks:
- Beyond digital formats, offering physical copies of your books in paperback or hardback appeals to readers who prefer tangible editions.

- It opens up opportunities for book signings, events, and physical distribution.

- For romance authors in particular, 'discreet covers' are becoming more popular lately as well

- Special edition covers:

  ○ Create limited or special editions of your books with unique covers, bonus content, or exclusive features.

  ○ This can attract collectors and dedicated fans, adding a premium revenue stream.

Audiobooks:
- Tap into the growing audiobook market by producing audio versions of your books.

- Audiobook platforms allow authors to reach a broader audience and generate additional income on content that you've already created.

- This is growing in popularity not only for the every day audiobook listener, but it's allowing people who might not be able to consume the written word to have access to your material in an inclusive way.

YouTube Channel:

- Explore content creation on platforms like YouTube, offering insights into your writing process, book reviews, or engaging discussions.

- Monetize your channel through ads, sponsorships, or Patreon integration.

Serialized Content:

- Release your stories in serialized formats, either independently or through platforms like Wattpad.

- This keeps readers eagerly anticipating the next installment and provides opportunities for monetization.

Patreon:

- Build a supportive community on Patreon by offering exclusive content, behind-the-scenes access, or personalized interactions with your fans.

- Subscriptions provide a consistent income stream.

Merchandise:

- Extend your brand with merchandise such as branded apparel, mugs, or other items related to your books.

- This not only generates revenue but also serves as additional marketing for your author brand.

Online Courses, Workshops, or Webinars:

- Leverage your expertise as an author (or a CPA *cough*) to offer online courses or workshops.

- Share insights on writing, self-publishing, or other relevant topics, creating an educational income stream.

Author Coaching or Consulting:

- Leverage your experience to provide coaching or consulting services for other authors.

- Offer guidance on writing, self-publishing, or building an author platform.

Collaborations and Anthologies:

- Participate in collaborative projects or contribute to anthologies.

- This not only diversifies your authorship but also introduces your work to new audiences.

Licensing and Adaptations:
- Explore opportunities for licensing your work for adaptations into movies, TV shows, or other media.

- This can result in substantial income and increased visibility.

- Be cautious of anyone who reaches out TO you about those rights. Please research to confirm the legitimacy before diving right in. Many author sites will help you figure out ways to tell if it's legitimate.

  - Sometimes it's suggested to not call the number on the email or letter but instead, find the company online (after figuring out it's legit, of course), and calling into their listed main line and asking about the communications you received.

Crowdfunding:
- Consider crowdfunding platforms like Kickstarter or Indiegogo to fund specific projects or book releases. Engage your audience and offer unique incentives for backers.

- Brandon Sanderson's campaign ring any bells? If not, look that up. It was record-setting.

Author Events and Speaking Engagements:
- Participate in book signings, literary festivals, or conferences as a speaker.

- Some events offer compensation or the opportunity to sell books directly to attendees.

  - On the flip side, many vendor events also charge vendor fees. Try to get a feel for the success of the event and how much you'd make after buying author copies to sell.

  - Just because the vendor fee was $20 and you sold $30 worth of books, doesn't mean you made a profit. You still had to buy (and ship) those books to yourself in the first place so you had additional costs there too. So, take that into consideration on whether you want to do an event.

Affiliate Marketing:
- Promote products or services related to your niche through affiliate marketing.

- Earn commissions for every sale made through your unique affiliate link.

Writing for Magazines or Blogs:
- Contribute articles, essays, or guest posts to magazines, blogs, or online platforms.

- Some publications offer payment for your contributions (or maybe it's the free advertising you want)

Literary Grants and Awards:
- Apply for literary grants or awards.

- Winning or being shortlisted for prestigious awards *can* bring financial rewards and increased visibility.

Mobile Apps and Games:
- Collaborate with developers to create mobile apps or games based on your books or characters.

- This can generate income through app sales or in-app purchases.

Virtual Reality (VR) Experiences:
- Explore partnerships to develop virtual reality experiences based on your stories.

- This innovative approach can attract tech-savvy audiences.

Author Retreats or Workshops:
- Organize and host author retreats or writing workshops.

- Charge participants for attendance, offering a unique and immersive experience.

Licensing Artwork:
- If your books feature illustrations or artwork, consider licensing these images for use in various products, from prints to merchandise.

By diversifying your income streams, you not only increase your financial resilience but also engage with a broader audience.

CHAPTER 27

1099s

In the realm of writing, understanding your business requirements is essential for authors, because if you don't do what you're supposed to and are caught, the penalties can be rough.

One critical aspect is the 1099 form—a document that reports various types of income received by individuals who are not employees. You probably receive them from the places that pay you (Amazon, IngramSpark, etc)

But did you know that you also have a responsibility to issue them (when required) as well?

This chapter serves as a guide to understand and fulfill the responsibility of issuing 1099 forms—an essential task in your author business.

What is a 1099?

- Issuing 1099 forms is a legal obligation when payments are made to individuals who aren't considered employees.

  - It is used by you (the business) to show the expense that you paid to another business (self-employed person) that resulted in *their* income.

- It ensures transparency in financial transactions and aids both parties in meeting their tax obligations.

- In the writing industry, this can include royalty payments, freelance earnings, or other forms of income.

- 1099 forms are given to:

  - The IRS

    - Either electronically or via mail

  - The contractor themselves

  - And sometimes the state

- Businesses or individuals can use IRS-approved software or engage a tax professional to assist with filing these forms accurately and on time.

  ○ The IRS provides instructions, guidelines, and forms necessary for filing 1099s on their official website.

  ○ Many bookkeeping softwares (like QBO) can track and issue them for you as well.

- It's essential to stay updated with IRS regulations and requirements regarding 1099 filings.

Who Receives a 1099?
- **Independent contractors, freelancers, or individuals who are not employees and provide services to a business may receive a Form 1099-NEC (Nonemployee Compensation) if they've been paid $600 or more in a tax year.**

  ○ Key point #1: If the contractor themselves is a C-corp or S-Corp, they do not need to be issued a 1099 by you.

  ○ Key point #2: It is not for supplies purchased

    - If you paid a small print shop down the road from you $800 to do a print run of your books, even if the print shop is a sole-proprietorship, because you bought supplies for your business, you do not owe them a 1099.

- Some examples of people who might need to receive one from you: editors, narrators, cover designers, personal assistant, marketing company, etc.

- Ask each of your contractor's for a completed W9 and it will tell you what type of entity they are (and the information necessary for filing)

- **If you paid someone royalties and it was over $10, you'll need to give them a 1099-MISC rather than a 1099-NEC**

  ○ Note the lower threshold for royalties paid out, the different form used, and the different due dates (below)

- **Tip**: Issue one to attorneys paid more than $600, even if they are corporations

- **Another hot tip:** For payments made via payment apps such as PayPal *Business*, Square, etc., **the responsibility for reporting falls on the payment processor, not the payer.** These platforms are considered third-party settlement organizations (TPSOs).

- The payment processor is required to issue a Form 1099-K to the service provider based on their own requirements. You don't need to do anything more.

  - If the payment processor issues a Form 1099-K, the payer (business or individual) generally does not need to issue a separate Form 1099-NEC for the same payments.

    - This is because the payments are already reported by the payment processor on the Form 1099-K.

  - HOWEVER, if you're making payments to vendors using the TPSO's *personal* payments option, and not selecting business payments or for 'goods and services', it's important to note that the TPSO will not provide Form 1099-K. In the TPSO's system, it's now a 'personal' transaction. Therefore, you will have to issue the 1099 yourself, if required.

  - *As of right now, <u>Zelle</u> does not issue 1099s!* So if you paid someone via Zelle, you need to look into that because you may need to issue that person a 1099.

Types of 1099 Forms:
- **1099-NEC: Nonemployee Compensation**

  - Used to report payments of $600 or more made to freelancers, including writers, editors, or other independent contractors.

- **1099-MISC: Miscellaneous Income**

  - Historically used for reporting nonemployee compensation, it's now reserved for specific situations, like **royalty payments**, rent, or prize winnings.

    - So if you do a royalty share and paid someone their royalty piece...if you pad them over $10 (the threshold for royalty 1099 filing), they'll need a 1099-MISC

- Other 1099 Varieties:

  - Different versions of Form 1099 exist for various types of income, such as interest, dividends, or rent

Issuer's Responsibility:
- **Collecting W-9 Forms:**

  - Obtain a completed W-9 form from each payee, ensuring accurate information for 1099 preparation.

- **Filing Deadlines:**

  - 1099-MISC:

    - Deadline for furnishing Copy B of Form 1099-MISC to recipients: generally by January 31 following the tax year.

    - Deadline for filing Copy A of Form 1099-MISC with the IRS: generally by the end of February (if filing by mail), or by the end of March (if filing electronically).

  - 1099-NEC:

    - Deadline for filing and furnishing to the recipients and the IRS needs to be done by January 31 following the tax year end

  - The IRS may impose penalties ranging from $50 to hundreds per form for inaccuracies or late filing.

    - However, if the failure to file or furnish is determined to be intentional or the result of willful neglect, the penalties can be substantially higher.

What is on a 1099?
- The 1099 will show:

  - Your information (name, address, SSN/EIN)

  - The recipient's name, address, Taxpayer Identification Number (TIN) or Social Security Number

  - And the total amount you paid for their services during the tax year

CHAPTER 28

What can I deduct and where do I put it?

This list is not exhaustive, but this is my opinion on the various categories and what goes in them.
If you're a larger entity who is tracking Cost of Goods Sold and Inventory, then you'll probably build the
"book production costs" into your COGS, but for the authors who operate on a Schedule C cash basis, I
think this is a good breakdown

* **Advertising**

  * Costs for promoting the business

  * Advertising costs (online ads, book promotions)

    * Facebook ads, amazon ads, TikTok ads, etc

  * Promotional materials, swag, giveaways

  * Website maintenance, hosting fees, newsletter services *(could be put under office expense)*

  * Book launch event expenses

  * Some charitable donations may qualify if there is an advertising component - ask your preparer

* **Car and Truck Expenses**

  * Vehicle-related expenses for business use

  * You'll probably just track mileage, but if so, keep track of total mileage and business mileage

    * Set a reminder at 1/1 to get your odometer reading every year and a log book to track your business miles.

- **Commissions**

  - Agent commissions

- **Contract Labor**

  - Payments to contractors or freelancers.

  - Royalty payments to co-authors or contributors

    - Make sure you're issuing 1099s as appropriate

      - $600 threshold for services; $10 threshold for royalties

- **Depreciation and Section 179 Expense Deduction**

  - Depreciation of business assets

    - *Usually calculated by your accountant/tax software*

- **Employee Benefits Program**

  - Costs for employee benefit programs

  - Employee health insurance

- **Insurance**

  - *Business* insurance premiums (not your health or life ins)

  - Professional liability insurance

- **Interest**

  - Interest on business loans or credit cards.

  - Not your home mortgage int or student loan interest

- **Legal and Professional Services**

  - Legal or accounting fees for the business

  - Legal advice or fees related to contracts or intellectual property rights

  - CPA or tax preparation fees

  - Payroll processing fees

  - Virtual Assistant/personal assistant

  - Bookkeeper

- **Office Expenses**

  - Supplies and expenses related to the business office

  - Stationery and Supplies

    - Pens, pencils, notebooks, notepads, paper, envelopes, sticky notes, and other writing materials.

  - Printer and Printer Supplies

    - Printer, ink or toner, paper, printer maintenance kits, and cartridges.

  - Computers

    - Computers, laptops, tablets

    - Monitors/keyboards/mouses/mousepads

  - Office Furniture

    - Desks, chairs, filing cabinets, bookshelves, or other furniture used exclusively for author work

    - Any office equipment/furniture that costs less than $2,500

  - Office Decor

    - Artwork, plants, or decorations enhancing the office ambiance.

- Reference Materials

  - Books, magazines, online subscriptions, or reference materials relevant to writing, research, or professional development.

  - This handbook...

- Shipping Supplies

  - Envelopes, packaging materials, postage stamps, and shipping labels for mailing manuscripts or promotional materials.

- Office Cleaning Supplies

  - Cleaning agents, trash bags, wipes, or other supplies used to maintain a clean workspace.

- Organization and Storage

  - Folders, binders, dividers, filing systems, or storage boxes to keep manuscripts or documents organized.

- Professional Memberships or Subscriptions

  - Membership fees for writing organizations, subscriptions to writing-related magazines, or online platforms.

- *Promotional Materials*

  - *Business cards, flyers, bookmarks, or promotional items used for marketing books or author brand.*

  - *Though, this could also be under advertising (pick a place that makes sense to you and be consistent)*

- Software Subscriptions

  - Writing-related subscriptions such as grammar checkers, cloud storage services, or project management tools.

- *Website Expenses*

  - *Domain registration, hosting fees, website design or maintenance costs for an author website or blog.*

- *Though, again, this could also be under advertising expense*

- **Pension and Profit-Sharing Plans**

  - Your contributions to *employee* retirement plan

  - For employees' retirements, NOT YOURS

    - Your contributions to any retirement plans go on your 1040 in a different place, not on the schedule C

    - Same with your health insurance premiums - those don't go on your Schedule C

    - You can subtotal them and give them to your accountant to take elsewhere though!

    - Both your health insurance premiums and your dental premiums

- **Rent or Lease**

  - Rental expenses for business property

  - Office rent, equipment rents

- **Repairs and Maintenance**

  - Costs for repairing or maintaining business property

  - Laptop repairs

  - Office furniture repairs

- **Supplies**

  - Costs of materials or supplies used in the business.

  - Or you could decide to make a 'Book Production Cost' category under the 'Miscellaneous Category' - your choice.

- **Taxes and Licenses**

- Business-related taxes or licenses

- Payroll taxes

- Sales taxes

- VAT

- State business taxes

- **Travel**

  - Travel expenses for book signings, author events, or conferences

  - Registration fees for writing workshops or conferences

  - Travel expenses for research purposes

- **Meals**

  - Business-related meal expenses

  - This is usually limited to 50% deductible

- **Utilities**

  - Costs for *business* utilities (electricity, phone, etc.) if you have a rented office or a *second* phone line that goes into your house

  - If you work from home and have a home office, then the utilities go in *that* section (not here)

    - In my opinion, a converted shed out back of your home, counts as a home office unless it has its own meter, internet, phone, etc.

  - **Hot tip: I recommend combining all types of utilities together in one 'Utilities' bucket.**

    - E.g. - Electricity, oil, sewer, water, internet, phone, etc. - can all go into one 'Utilities' bucket rather than splitting them all out on their own lines

    - No need to overcomplicate things

- **Wages**

  - Employee wages or salaries.

  - Schedule C:

    - Again - not your *Draw* if you're filing a Schedule C - you may take a 'draw' but it is not an expense for your business. Again, the IRS doesn't even want to know what you put in or took out of your business on your tax return. Instead, you're just taxed on the net income after expenses are taken out, regardless of whether you took that money out for your own purposes or not.

  - S or C Corps:

    - Split out your wages from any employee wages

- **Other Expenses** (*You have the ability to create your own categories of expenses under "other expenses". Just try not to go too crazy with it. Try to fit it into an established category if you can.*)

  - **Miscellaneous expenses**

    - Reconciliation discrepancies

    - Contest or award entry fees

    - Research expenses

    - Bad debt - you paid someone who ghosted you

      - Tip – just because they ghosted you, doesn't mean they are now ineligible for a 1099 filing requirement. The IRS has instructions on how to submit a 1099 for a person who is...uncooperative...with your requests for their information for 1099 filing. Give it a look on irs.gov

    - *These misc expenses can sometimes be put into 'Office expense' depending on what they are*

  - **Professional Development**

    - Writing courses or workshops

    - Membership fees for writing associations or groups

- Coaching or mentoring fees

- **Book Production Costs:** (*This could also be argued as Supplies or Cost of Goods Sold but I personally like them here*)

  - Copyright registration fees

  - Editors: developmental editing, copyediting, line editing, proofreading, etc (though these could fall under *Contract Labor*)

  - Alpha reader and beta readers

  - Cover designer fees

  - Book formatting services

  - ISBN purchases

  - Printing and distribution costs *(could be under supplies or COGS)*

  - Audiobook production fees

  - Etc.

Hopefully that helps!
Also, side note, don't pay for reviews

CHAPTER 29

Ghosted

But wait! What if my designer / editor / etc. ghosted me and I paid for the service/goods but didn't actually get anything? Can I still deduct that expense?

Yes!

You are cash basis and it's cash you put out for the sake of your business. Just because it turned out to be a bad expense, doesn't mean that you can't take it as an expense.

Put that puppy down as a deduction. Make note though, you still may be required to issue them a 1099. If they refuse to share that information with you, some do, you can follow the steps on the IRS website.

CHAPTER 30

High level: where do things go on a Schedule C

We somewhat did this already but here's another high-level look (some accounts are removed for simplicity)
Income:

- Royalties

- Direct Sales Income

- Audiobook Income

- Other income

You can combine your income sources on one gross receipts line if you want, you don't need to break them out per payer or per type of income.

Expenses:

- Advertising: Costs for promoting the business.

- Car and Truck Expenses: Vehicle-related expenses for business use.

- Commissions and Fees: Payments made to others for services rendered.

- Contract Labor: Payments to contractors or freelancers.

- Depreciation and Section 179 Expense Deduction: Depreciation of business assets.

- Employee Benefits Program: Costs for employee benefit programs.

- Insurance: Business insurance premiums (not health or life)

- Interest: Interest on business loans or credit cards.

- Legal and Professional Services: Legal or accounting fees for the business.

- Office Expenses: Supplies and expenses related to the business office.

- Pension and Profit-Sharing Plans: Contributions to employee retirement plans. (for employees,

NOT YOU. Your contributions to any retirement plans go on your 1040 in a different place, not on the schedule C. Same with your health insurance)

- Rent or Lease: Rental expenses for business property.

- Repairs and Maintenance: Costs for repairing or maintaining business property.

- Supplies: Costs of materials or supplies used in the business.

- Taxes and Licenses: Business-related taxes or licenses

- Travel, Meals, and Entertainment: Business-related travel and meal expenses.

- Utilities: Costs for business utilities (electricity, phone, etc.).

- Wages: Employee wages or salaries.

- Other Expenses:

  - Miscellaneous expenses not listed in specific categories.

CHAPTER 31

High level: where do things go on Form 1065

Some accounts are removed for simplicity

Income:

- Royalties

- Direct Sales Income

- Audiobook Income

- Other income

You can combine your income sources on one gross receipts line if you want, you don't need to break them out per payer or per type of income.

Expenses:

- Salaries and wages: Payments made to employees

- Guaranteed payments to partners: Payments made to partners/members per operating agreements

- Repairs and maintenance: Costs for repairing or maintaining business property.

- Rent or Lease: Rental expenses for business property.

- Taxes and licenses: Business-related taxes or licenses.

- Interest expense: Interest paid on business loans or credit.

- Depreciation and amortization: Depreciation of business assets.

- Other deductions: Miscellaneous deductions not categorized elsewhere.

CHAPTER 32

High level: where do things go on Form 1120/S

Some accounts are removed for simplicity

Income:

- Royalties

- Direct Sales Income

- Audiobook Income

- Other income

You can combine your income sources on one gross receipts line if you want, you don't need to break them out per payer or per type of income.

Expenses:

- Compensation of officers: Wages and salaries paid to corporate officers (you, probably)

- Salaries and wages: what you paid to employees

- Repairs and maintenance: cost to fix equipment, etc

- Rent and lease expenses: Rental or lease costs for business property.

- Taxes and licenses: Business-related taxes or licenses.

- Interest: any credit card or loan interest, etc

- Depreciation and amortization: Depreciation of corporate assets.

- Advertising: Costs to promote your business

- Pension, profit-sharing, etc., plans: Any amounts paid for retirement

- Employee benefit programs: Any payments made for things like employee health insurance, etc

- Other deductions: Miscellaneous deductions not categorized elsewhere.

CHAPTER 33

Mileage and auto

Businesses or individuals using vehicles for business purposes can deduct related expenses on their tax returns.

Methods are: actual expenses or mileage deductions (commonly used for simplicity).

If a vehicle is used for both personal and business purposes, only the portion used for business qualifies for deductions.

To claim deductions, individuals or businesses must meet IRS requirements, maintain detailed records, and accurately document the business use of the vehicle.

Special rules may apply to specific situations, such as leased vehicles, vehicles used by employees, or vehicles used for multiple purposes (personal, business, charitable, or medical).

Tax tip: Make a note on your calendar to grab your odometer at 12/31 every year. From year to year, you can now see your total miles driven (the difference in the odometer), and if you tracked your business mileage, then you find the difference between your total miles and your business miles to get your personal miles. Easy peasy. Give this information to your tax preparer (or enter it yourself if you do your own taxes)

Methods

1. Actual Expenses Method:
* This method involves tracking and deducting actual costs associated with the vehicle, such as gas, maintenance, repairs, insurance, depreciation, lease payments (if applicable), and other related expenses.

2. Mileage Deduction Method (Standard Mileage Rate):
* The IRS offers a standard mileage rate, a set amount per mile driven for business purposes.

* For the tax year 2024, the standard mileage rate is 67 cents per mile driven for business use.

- To claim the mileage deduction, track the number of business miles driven throughout the year, including trips for business meetings, client visits, book fairs, speaking engagements, or other work-related travel.

- It's crucial to maintain accurate records for mileage or actual expenses.

  - This includes documenting dates, destinations, purposes of trips, and mileage logs to substantiate business use.

- Many people have a mileage log stored in their glove boxes.

  - Others have apps on their phones

CHAPTER 34

Home Office Deduction

As an author running your writing business from home, you might be eligible for the home office deduction, which allows you to deduct expenses associated with the portion of your home **used exclusively and regularly** for business purposes

Claiming the home office deduction can help reduce your taxable income, ultimately lowering your tax liability.

However, it's *essential* to understand and comply with IRS rules and requirements.

Remember, if you choose to deduct your home office space, you essentially get to depreciate part of your house for your business...which means you must reclaim that depreciation recapture if you sell your house later on. Keep an eye on that and discuss with your accountant. I've always been advised that it's depreciation allowed or *allowable* so even if your accountant doesn't take the depreciation expense for your home office, I was always taught that you still had to factor in what you *would have* taken for depreciation. Then again, I spoke with another person the other day who said that's not what they do...so...do with that what you will. Talk to a professional and look up IRS Form 8829 for the most up-to-date instructions.

Ok, so per the IRS:

"Whether you're self-employed or a partner, you may be able to deduct certain expenses for the part of your home that you use for business.

To deduct expenses for business use of the home, you must use part of your home as one of the following:

1. Exclusively on a regular basis as your principal place of business for your trade or business;

2. Exclusively on a regular basis as a place where you meet or deal with your patients, clients, or customers in the normal course of your trade or business;

3. A separate structure that's not attached to your home, used exclusively on a regular basis in connection with your trade or business;

4. On a regular basis for storage of inventory or product samples used in your trade or business of selling products at retail or wholesale, so long as your home is the sole fixed location of such trade or business;"

So I believe all that boils down to:

Exclusive and Regular Use:
- The space claimed for the home office deduction must be used "exclusively" for business purposes.

- It could be a room, a portion of a room, or a separate structure (like a studio) used regularly for business activities, such as writing, research, or administrative tasks.

- Don't have a spare bed in your 'home office'

Qualification Criteria:
- The area claimed must be the primary place where you conduct business, meet clients, or perform administrative tasks related to your writing business.

- It doesn't have to be a separate room but must be dedicated solely to business activities.

Types of Expenses Deductible:
- You can deduct direct expenses related to the home office, like painting or repairs specific to that space.

- **Additionally, a portion of indirect expenses—such as mortgage interest, property taxes, utilities, home insurance, home security, internet, and depreciation—can be deductible based on the percentage of your home used for business.**

Simplified Option:
- The IRS offers a simplified option where you can deduct $5 per square foot of your home used for business, up to a maximum of 300 square feet.

- This simplified method bypasses the detailed calculations of actual expenses and depreciation.

  ○ But even though it bypasses the depreciation calculation, I still believe you need to factor in the depreciation recapture when you sell your home. Check the IRS' site for guidance.

Documentation:
- Keep thorough records and documentation to support your home office deduction claim.

- This includes measurements of the office space, receipts for related expenses, and records showing the exclusive and regular use of that space for business.

Give your accountant the purchase price and date of your home (what was attributed to the land value and what was attributed to the building itself), the square footage of your home <u>and</u> the office space, your home mortgage interest (if any), property taxes paid (usually on the mortgage int statement Form 1098), and the yearly total of the items given above.

CHAPTER 35

Retirement Plans

Retirement plans are crucial but often overlooked by authors navigating the twists and turns of their literary careers.

Unfortunately, many of my clients over the years would always say they didn't have the cash flow to put money into a retirement account. I totally understood their standpoint, but I also felt worried that they were going to be seventy years old and living on nothing but their Social Security payments. Don't be that person. Don't be seventy and only receiving social security and royalty payments. Invest in your future if you can!

Here are a few of the more popular plans for authors but I'm not advising you one way or another.

This is my basic understanding of these plans, so please talk with a financial advisor – this is **not** my specialty!

Individual 401(k) (Solo 401(k)):
- This plan is designed for self-employed individuals or small business owners without employees (other than a spouse).

- It allows for higher contribution limits than some other plans, enabling both employer and employee contributions.

SEP-IRA (Simplified Employee Pension Individual Retirement Account):
- A SEP-IRA allows higher contribution limits than traditional IRAs and is suitable for sole proprietors or small businesses, including authors with fluctuating income, as contributions are flexible.

- However, if you have employees, know that the percents for funding usually have to be the same.

  - The same percentage of compensation applies uniformly to both eligible employees and the self-employed business owner when making contributions to a SEP IRA

    - If you want to contribute 10% of your net income to your SEP...you must contribute 10% of all eligible employee's salaries into into their SEP IRAs.

- Translated to = it can get expensive. Fast

- I see this as the most recommended plan in my area of the country though (usually when the business doesn't have employees)

SIMPLE IRA (Savings Incentive Match Plan for Employees):

- This plan is suitable for self-employed individuals with a small number of employees.

- Allows both employer and employee contributions.

- *CPAs like to say – there is nothing 'simple' about simple plans*

Traditional or Roth IRA (Individual Retirement Account):

- These are standard retirement accounts available to anyone with earned income.

  ◦ What if you hired your child and helped them set up their won IRA account...can you imagine what that would be valued at when they turned 65?

- Traditional IRAs offer tax-deferred growth, while Roth IRAs provide tax-free withdrawals in retirement and inheritance

Each retirement plan has its unique features, contribution limits, eligibility criteria, and tax implications.

Authors interested in setting up a retirement plan should consult with a financial advisor or tax professional to select the most suitable option based on their specific circumstances and financial objectives. There are deadlines to setting them up so make sure you plan ahead!

Whether you're just starting your writing career or have an established literary portfolio, understanding and implementing a retirement plan is a pivotal step towards financial independence

Chapter 36

Hiring your kids

When you employ your children in your writing business and pay them a reasonable wage for actual work performed, you can possibly enjoy some notable payroll tax benefits

For the purposes of this guidance, it is my understanding that the IRS considers a sole proprietorship to be the same as a SMLLC

See IRS page here for the most up-to-date information:
https://www.irs.gov/businesses/small-businesses-self-employed/family-help

---

If the business is a parent's *sole proprietorship* or a *partnership* in which each partner is a parent of the child:

- **No FICA (Social Security and Medicare) Taxes:**

  - If your child is under 18, their wages for working in your business **are exempt** from FICA taxes (Social Security and Medicare).

    - This exemption *applies to both* the employer and the employee portion of these taxes.

  - Payments for the services of a child under age 21 **are not subject** to Federal Unemployment Act (FUTA) tax.

    - If the child is 21 years or older, then payments for the services of a child **are subject** to FUTA taxes.

If the business is a corporation, a partnership (unless each partner is a parent of the child), or an estate (even if it is the estate of the deceased parent of the child):

- Payments for services of a child **are subject** to income tax withholding, social security taxes, Medicare taxes and FUTA taxes regardless of age.

- **Income Tax Deduction for the Business:**

  - You can deduct the wages you pay to your child as a business expense on your tax return.

  - This reduces your business's taxable income, potentially lowering your overall tax liability.

- **Lower Tax Bracket for the Child:**

  - If your child earns below the standard deduction threshold (for 2023, it's $12,950 for a single filer), they might not owe federal income taxes.

  - This means they could potentially receive their wages tax-free.

- **Education Savings:**

  - You can use their earnings to fund a Roth IRA (or Traditional IRA, though I recommend Roth) or contribute to a college savings plan, helping them start building savings or preparing for future educational/retirement expenses.

- To qualify for these tax benefits, it's crucial that the work your child performs for your business is legitimate and that you pay them a reasonable wage for the services rendered.

- Keep detailed records of their work, hours, and payments to support their employment.

Always consult with a tax professional or accountant to ensure compliance with tax regulations and to maximize the tax advantages of hiring your kids in your writing business.

CHAPTER 37

Hiring other family members

Maybe you want to hire family members who aren't your kids. There a some advantages to this...
Let's explore.

Hiring <u>your</u> <u>spouse</u> when you are a sole proprietorship

- If your spouse is your employee, not your partner, the wages **are subject** to Social Security and Medicare taxes for him/her **but not FUTA tax.**

Be careful that you are not 'partners' in the business. If you are, then you're looking at a 1065 Partnership Return, or maybe a qualified joint venture. Talk to your accountant.
https://www.irs.gov/businesses/small-businesses-self-employed/married-couples-in-business

---

Hiring <u>your</u> <u>parent</u> when you are a sole proprietorship

- Payments for services of a parent **are subject** to income tax withholding, social security taxes and Medicare taxes *but* **not subject** *to FUTA tax*

Hiring <u>your</u> <u>parent</u> when your business is a corporation (even if controlled by the you), a partnership (even if you are a partner), or an estate:

- The payments for the services of a parent **are subject** to income tax withholding, social security taxes, Medicare taxes and FUTA taxes.

Benefits of hiring family members

- Deductible business expense:

  - Paying a family member for legitimate work done for your business allows you to deduct their wages as a business expense.

  - This reduces your taxable income, ultimately lowering your tax liability.

- If the family member is in a lower tax bracket, this can reduce the overall taxes owed on the income they earn from your business.

  - Shifting income from your higher tax bracket to your family member's lower tax bracket can result in overall tax savings

- Retirement and health benefits:

  - Employing family members can also enable them to participate in retirement plans or health benefits offered by your business, potentially saving on taxes because it's deductible for you, and providing them with valuable benefits.

However, it's crucial to ensure that the family member is legitimately working for your business and that the wages paid are reasonable for the services performed.

Keep accurate records of their work, hours, and payments to substantiate their employment.

Always consult with a tax professional or accountant to ensure compliance with tax regulations and to maximize the tax advantages of hiring your family members in your writing business.

CHAPTER 38

Publishing company umbrella

What if you want to publish not only your books, but other peoples' books too?
That's totally fine. Get a contract in writing!

Just remember, if you publish them via your KDP account (or other platform), then the royalties will show up on *your* author dashboard.

You'll then remit the royalties to the author per whatever royalty agreement you have in place.

At year end, **you will issue them a 1099-MISC** reflecting the royalty amounts sent to them. This will remove their income from your business net income, basically zeroing out the income against the expense on your income statement. Therefore, you will not have to pay income taxes on the income that you then distributed out to the other authors.

The same strategy applies if you write with a co-writer.

Generally, you could put these payments under the "contract labor" expense bucket, though you could create a separate expense under 'other expenses' if it helps your brain to group them separately.

CHAPTER 39

*Audiobook Creation and the ADA

I hesitated to even add this chapter as I have no personal experience in this matter and this is simply based on conversations I've been hearing from other accountants.

Audiobooks are audio recordings of written material, providing an accessible format for individuals who prefer or require auditory content.

FULL DISCLOSURE: THIS SECTION IS NOT BLACK AND WHITE. YOU MUST DISCUSS WITH YOUR ACCOUNTANT BEFORE MOVING FORWARD WITH THIS STRATEGY. I SIMPLY WANTED TO MAKE SURE I ADDRESSED THE CURRENT CONVERSATIONS CIRCULATING TO <u>PROMPT A DISCUSSION AND FURTHER RESEARCH.</u>

For detailed guidance on ADA compliance in audiobook distribution, consulting legal professionals or accessibility experts can provide specific strategies to ensure compliance with ADA standards.

I recommend that you consult with an attorney who specializes in ADA compliance issues to see whether the ADA even applies to audiobook products.

While the Americans with Disabilities Act (ADA) doesn't specifically address audiobooks, it underscores the importance of accessibility, encouraging consideration for individuals with disabilities in the distribution and availability of audiobooks across various platforms and institutions.

Americans with Disabilities Act (ADA):
- The ADA mandates accessibility for individuals with disabilities, ensuring equal access to goods, services, and communications.

- Again – The ADA doesn't explicitly address audiobooks

- Offering audiobooks *could* align with ADA principles by providing accessible content for individuals with visual impairments or other disabilities that hinder reading printed material.

Disabled Access Credit:
- Provides a non-refundable credit of up to $5,000 for small businesses that incur expenditures for the purpose of providing access to persons with disabilities.

- See here – https://www.eeoc.gov/fact-sheet/facts-about-disability-related-tax-provisions

- To minimize any potential he said/she said, I'm going to quote the IRS instruction page exactly for *Form 8826: Disabled Access Credit*

"Purpose of the Form: Eligible small businesses use Form 8826 to claim the disabled access credit. This credit is part of the general business credit.

Taxpayers, other than partnerships or S corporations, whose only source of this credit is from those pass-through entities, are not required to complete or file this form. Instead, they can report this credit directly on Form 3800.

Eligible Access Expenditures: For purposes of the credit, these expenditures are amounts paid or incurred by the eligible small business to comply with applicable requirements under the Americans With Disabilities Act of 1990 (Public Law 101-336) as in effect on November 5, 1990. Eligible access expenditures include amounts paid or incurred:

1. To remove barriers that prevent a business from being accessible to or usable by individuals with disabilities;

2. To provide qualified interpreters or other methods of making audio materials available to hearing-impaired individuals;

3. *To provide qualified readers, taped texts, and other methods of making visual materials available to individuals with visual impairments;* or

4. To acquire or modify equipment or devices for individuals with disabilities."

- Audiobook creation and ADA

  - The Disabled Access Credit (DAC) under Section 44 of the IRS Code is designed to assist small businesses in complying with the Americans with Disabilities Act (ADA) by making their establishments more accessible to individuals with disabilities.

○ While this credit isn't directly aimed at audiobook creation, it _could_ potentially apply if the expenses incurred in your business relate to enhancing accessibility for individuals with disabilities, including aspects of audiobook distribution or related services.

○ Small businesses with either total revenues of $1 million or less in the previous tax year or fewer than 30 full-time employees during the last tax year could possibly claim this credit.

○ Expenses associated with making the business more accessible, such as renovations for ramps, accessible entrances, restroom modifications, signage improvements, or technology enhancements for accessibility, may qualify for the credit.

○ The credit is equal to 50% of eligible expenses up to $10,250 for a maximum credit of $5,000 per year. Eligible businesses can claim this credit against their federal income tax liability.

This credit is treated differently based on your entity type, so keep that in mind as well.

It's crucial to consult with a tax professional to determine the specific eligibility of expenses related to audiobook distribution or accessibility enhancements for the Disabled Access Credit. They can provide tailored guidance based on your business expenses and efforts to comply with ADA regulations.

CHAPTER 40

*Value-Added Tax (VAT) and Goods and Services Tax

<u>This is all in generalities because I'm not a tax specialist, nor do I want to become one...</u>

- Value-Added Tax (VAT) is a type of sales tax that some countries charge on the <u>*purchase*</u> of goods and services. In fact, more than 170 countries, including all European countries, have VATs.

- It's a bit different from the sales tax in the United States.

  - With VAT, each step of the production and sales process adds a bit of tax.

  - Ultimately though, the end consumer is the one who pays the total tax ("output tax").

  - The other businesses along the way get tax credits for when they pay their step's VAT ("input taxes").

- VAT rates and rules can vary from country to country.

  - Some countries have high VAT rates, some have lower ones, and some exempt books from VAT altogether.

- For the purpose of VATs, historically ebooks and books have been treated differently.

  - For instance, physical books in the UK were zero-rated items which made them not subject to VAT. However, they did have a VAT on ebooks. In 2020, the UK dropped the VAT on ebooks but it goes to show that some countries do view them as separate items.

- There is a portal on the EU government pages for each country called *Import One-Stop Shop* in the European Union which can act as a centralized hub for your VAT tracking with the goal to simplify the declaration and payments of VATs in the EU.

- Another thing that is headache-inducing is the fact that these various countries have different deadlines/timelines for collecting, remitting, and filing the taxes/forms.

- Ultimately, you need to look at the thresholds for each of these countries to see if you maybe are incurring VAT and you didn't even realize it.

- You can also look up the long-distance selling for nexus thresholds/guidance

---

Some extra notes:
- Goods and Services Tax (GST) (not the GST in the US, which is Generation Skipping tax) is a type of tax that is imposed on the _cost_ of goods and services.

  ○ This is also levied at each step in the supply chain, however this is usually a flat-rate percent.

- When you start researching your intended foreign country, also make sure to look up any import duties or tariffs

- My experience – when I sell direct internationally, I use selling platforms/apps that manage those reporting/tax requirements for me so I don't have to try to keep track of a million different rules. My time is valuable and that small percent of my sales for them to manage this for me is worth every penny.

I am not an international tax expert, so I can't speak further on this filing requirement and what it entails for you as an author. I also don't _want_ to be an expert on this. I'm happy letting other people much more knowledgable handle these requirements and instruct/advise others.

If you are doing direct sales in foreign countries, make sure you find an international tax specialist who can help. Also, be prepared for a big tax bill – they're a specialist for a reason and their knowledge is _hard_ to come by.

CHAPTER 41

*Direct Sales

Direct sales – the bane of *this* CPA's existence...and the joy of an author's.

Direct sales have emerged as a powerful avenue for connecting with readers and maximizing revenue. This chapter delves into the nuances of direct sales, providing insights and strategies for authors keen on exploring this dynamic channel.

- When doing Direct Sales, you open yourself up to:

    ○ Foreign Reporting/Taxes

    ○ Sales (and Use) Tax Nexus

    ○ Income Tax Nexus

Let's start from the beginning...

Understanding Direct Sales:

- **Definition:**

    ○ Direct sales involve authors selling their books directly to readers, bypassing traditional retail channels.

    ○ This can occur through various platforms, including author websites, events, and social media.

- **Benefits:**

    ○ Direct sales offer authors higher profit margins and direct engagement with their audience.

    ○ It provides an avenue to build a loyal reader base and gather valuable feedback.

- ○ And *much* more but that's not what you're reading this book for

Some Platforms for Direct Sales:
- **Author Websites:**

  - ○ Building a user-friendly online store on your author website allows readers to purchase books directly, creating a seamless transaction experience.

- **Social Media:**

  - ○ Utilizing platforms like Facebook, Instagram, TikTok, or Twitter enables authors to showcase and sell their books directly to engaged followers.

- **Events and Conventions:**

  - ○ Author participation in events, book fairs, or conventions allows for face-to-face sales, personalized signings, and connection-building.

Logistics and Considerations:
- **Payment Processing:**

  - ○ Setting up secure and efficient payment processing systems is crucial.

  - ○ Explore options like PayPal, Stripe, or dedicated e-commerce solutions.

  - ○ Some software platforms track, withhold, and file sales taxes for you. Others simply track. Find what works best for you

- **Inventory Management:**

  - ○ Maintain accurate inventory records to fulfill orders promptly.

  - ○ Implementing inventory management systems streamlines this process.

  - ○ *Once you hit a certain point,* the IRS may require you to start reporting your year's beginning inventory, your year's ending inventory, and what you bought and sold for inventory *during* the year.

    - This is on your Schedule C under 'Cost of Goods Sold'

Legal and Tax Implications:
- **Sales Tax Compliance:**

  - Authors engaging in direct sales must navigate sales tax obligations.

  - Understanding and complying with state-specific regulations is essential.

    - There are also some areas with local sales taxes – use the power of the internet to make sure you're adhering to local codes

  - We have a chapter on Sales Taxes.

- **Foreign Reporting/Taxes on International Sales**

  - We have a chapter on this though I'm not an international tax specialist, so it's simply an overview to prompt meaningful thought and discussion with someone much smarter than me.

- **Record keeping:**

  - Thorough record keeping of direct sales transactions is crucial for accurate financial reporting and tax preparation.

Direct sales empower authors to take control of their revenue streams and deepen connections with readers.

By navigating the logistics, legal aspects, and crafting a robust strategy, authors can harness the full potential of direct sales in their entrepreneurial journey.

CHAPTER 42

*Direct Sales: Foreign Reporting/Taxes

Understanding Foreign Taxes, VAT, and EU Regulations for Direct Sales:

Navigating global sales involves understanding and complying with diverse tax regulations, VAT requirements, and legal considerations.

Authors expanding their reach to international markets should proactively seek professional guidance to ensure legal and tax compliance, fostering a successful and legally sound global sales strategy.

I am NOT an international tax specialist. Take what I have here as generalities learned from my experience and research, and find someone who specializes in this to discuss further.

- **Global Sales Tax Overview:**

    ○ Authors engaging in direct sales to international customers must consider various tax implications, including foreign taxes, Value Added Tax (VAT), and compliance with European Union (EU) regulations.

- **Value Added Tax (VAT):**

    ○ Many countries, especially those in the EU, impose VAT on the sale of goods.

    ○ Authors should be aware of VAT thresholds in each country and *register for VAT if their sales surpass these thresholds.*

- **VAT Rates and Compliance:**

    ○ Different countries have varying VAT rates.

    ○ Authors should research and understand the applicable rates for the regions where they sell books.

    ○ Compliance involves charging the correct VAT, collecting it from customers, and remitting it to the respective tax authorities.

- **EU Distance Selling Rules:**

  - The EU has specific regulations known as Distance Selling Rules that apply to cross-border sales within the EU.

  - Authors may need to register for VAT in EU member states based on their sales volume to customers in each country.

- **Digital Services Tax (DST):**

  - Some countries implement Digital Services Tax on online sales.

  - Authors should stay informed about the jurisdictions where these taxes apply and assess whether their sales trigger DST obligations.

Legal Considerations for Global Sales:
- **International Contractual Agreements:**

  - Authors should review and update their sales terms and conditions to address international sales.

  - Clearly communicate shipping costs, delivery times, and potential taxes to customers.

- **Customs Declarations and Duties:**

  - Authors must accurately complete customs declarations for international shipments.

  - Customers may be responsible for paying import duties, and authors should provide transparent information about these potential charges.

- **Data Protection Regulations:**

  - Adhere to international data protection regulations, such as the General Data Protection Regulation (GDPR) in the EU.

  - Ensure that customer data is handled in compliance with applicable laws.

Professional Guidance and Compliance:
- **Consult with Tax Professionals:**

  - Seek advice from international tax specialists who can provide insights into specific tax obligations in different countries.

- Full disclosure again (can you tell I'm doing my best not to get sued?), I am NOT an expert in foreign sales. All of this is what I know *in theory*, but I very well might be missing valuable chunks of information. The six and seven figure authors I know, many do not currently report any foreign sales tax information on their direct sales. Several actually don't allow any international direct sales at all, just because of the sheer level of complexity. However, there are several platforms that will act as the middle-man of sorts for you

- **Utilize E-commerce Platforms:**

  - Consider using e-commerce platforms with built-in features for managing international sales, including automated tax calculations and compliance tools.

  - Basically, these platforms will become the 'sellers on record' more or less, and they'll be the ones calculating and remitting those taxes. There will be some percentage fee for this service, but after they take their cut, they will then send you your portion of the sale.

    - Similar to how Amazon handles international sales. They sell your ebooks to people in Germany, but you aren't paying Germany taxes, Amazon is. You're just getting the payment and then receiving a 1099 at year-end as Amazon's contractor.

CHAPTER 43

*Direct Sales: Sales Tax

Historically, sales tax has been charged on tangible property, but a growing number of states are taxing various services.

They are also moving into intangible property, such as *digital downloads* of music, *books*, and movies

―――――――――――

Sales and Use Taxes

- As of this writing, forty-five states and the District of Columbia impose sales and use taxes.

- The following five states do not impose sales and use taxes (currently):

  ○ Alaska (local governments are allowed to impose sales taxes);

  ○ Delaware (imposes statewide business license tax and use tax);

  ○ Montana;

  ○ New Hampshire

  ○ Oregon

- Companies that have **sales tax <u>nexus</u>** are responsible for collecting sales tax on any sales made in (or to) that state (on the products or services that are subject to sales tax) (things that generate nexus are discussed shortly), but high level:

  ○ For example, you might go to an in-person signing in a state that has sales taxes on books. Check their threshold for filing and remitting sales taxes, because there's a good chance you need to register with that state (before you even go and make those sales) and then file those sales taxes after the event. Each state has their own rates and filing schedules so either do your research, or find an app that will do it for you.

  ○ **What if you sell online to residents of a certain state?**

- Companies that have sales tax nexus are responsible for collecting sales tax on any sales **made to residents of that state** (for products or services that are subject to sales tax).

  - I.E. – if you live in Vermont but you make a lot of online sales to customers/readers in Massachusetts, keep track of the number of sales made (to the residents of MA), and the cumulative yearly total, so you can know when you should be collecting, filing, and remitting sales tax

- **PLEASE NOTE: With online sales, it's determined by where the customer lives. Not you or your business location.**

- If you don't collect the tax, either because you didn't know you were supposed to or because you chose not to, the state does not care — You'll be in trouble.

  - Ignorance of the law is not a good excuse

CHAPTER 44

*Direct Sales: Sales Tax and Inventory Purchases

When purchasing inventory for direct sales, authors must be aware of sales tax implications. Sales tax is typically levied on the sale of tangible goods and varies by state.

Tax-Exempt Status:
- Some authors may qualify for tax-exempt status when buying inventory.

- This exemption is often available for resale businesses, and authors should explore obtaining a resale certificate from their state's tax authority.

Exception Statements for Inventory Purchases:
- Resale Certificate:

  - A resale certificate allows authors to buy inventory without paying sales tax upfront.

  - Instead, they collect and remit sales tax when selling the books directly to consumers.

- Verification of Exemption:

  - Authors should ensure that their exemption is valid for the specific type of goods they are purchasing.

  - States may have different rules regarding exempt items.

Compliance and Reporting:
- Record keeping:

- Maintain detailed records of inventory purchases, including invoices and resale certificates.

- This documentation is essential for sales tax compliance and may be requested during audits

- State-Specific Regulations:

    - Different states have varying rules on sales tax exemptions for inventory.

    - Authors should familiarize themselves with the specific regulations in their state to ensure compliance.

Filing Sales Tax Returns:
- Collection and Remittance:

    - Authors collect sales tax from buyers at the time of the sale (or work it into their price)

    - This tax must then be remitted to the appropriate state tax authority.

- Frequency of Filing:

    - The frequency of sales tax filing depends on the author's sales volume.

    - Some states require monthly filings, while others may permit quarterly or annual filings.

Sales Tax Software and Solutions:
- Automation Tools:

    - Consider utilizing sales tax automation software to streamline the calculation, collection, and remittance process.

    - These tools help authors stay compliant with changing tax rates.

- Professional Guidance:

    - Authors should seek guidance from tax professionals or accountants familiar with the intricacies of sales tax in the specific states where they conduct business.

Navigating sales tax in direct sales involves understanding exemption rules, maintaining meticulous records, and staying informed about state-specific regulations. Or...paying someone to do that for you

CHAPTER 45

*Direct Sales: Nexus

Nexus. What is it? How do I know if I have it? Is it contagious? How do you treat it?

- **What is Nexus?**

  - **It's a connection or sufficient presence that a business or individual has within a particular state or jurisdiction, which triggers tax obligations in that location.**

- Each state has different nexus requirements (remember, this is why you pay your CPA in gold bars and firstborns)

- It's important to be aware of nexus rules because they determine where and how you might need to pay taxes based on your business activities.

  - You also might be required to get a sales tax permit in those areas

---

Different Relevant Nexus Types:

Economic Nexus Test:
- **This test considers solely the volume of sales into a state, irrespective of physical presence.**

- **Once a business exceeds a certain sales threshold, nexus is established** (usually it's $100,000-$200,000 in sales, but it varies state to state, please verify)

Sales Threshold Test:
- **Meeting a certain level of sales within a state, either in terms of revenue or number of transactions, can create nexus.**

- **This threshold varies by state** (usually it's 100-200 transactions, though it varies, please verify)

Physical Presence Test:

- Nexus can be established if a business has a physical presence in the state, such as a store, office, warehouse, or employees working there.

Employee Test:

- Having employees working in the state may create nexus, even if the business doesn't have a physical location there.

Click-Through Nexus:

- This occurs when a business contracts with in-state residents who refer customers via a website link, creating a connection triggering nexus.

Marketplace Nexus:

- For businesses selling through online marketplaces, the use of a marketplace located in a state might create nexus.

CHAPTER 46

Direct Sales and Online Sales

Let's walk through this with an example...

Ok, so you're jumping on the 'selling direct' train.

You now sell your books online through your website.

Nexus is like a connection between your book sales and a specific state. When your book sales reach a certain level, or when you have a significant number of customers from a particular state, it creates a responsibility for you to follow that state's tax rules.

Let's say you live and operate your business from State A, but you sell a considerable number of books and/or ebooks to readers in State B through your website. If your sales in State B reach a specific threshold or if you start storing inventory there, you might establish nexus in State B. This means you might need to collect sales tax from your readers in State B and send it to that state's tax authority. *It also might be you have to file and report revenue in that state and pay income taxes there (income tax nexus).*

Check each state to see if they consider the deliverable of nontangible goods like ebooks or audiobooks towards their filing thresholds, or if they just count physical goods delivered.

You might be thinking...."Wait! I have no idea where my customers are when I sell through a place like Amazon!"

- Generally, Amazon is responsible for collecting and remitting the sales tax from the transactions. That's why you receive a 1099 at year-end. They're the seller on record, not you.

- Research the Wayfair legal case for the big precedent of the century if you want to geek out.

  - In response to Wayfair, these marketplace nexus laws incorporate a minimum transaction number and/or sales amount before the marketplace facilitator (you) is liable for sales tax

  - Currently, all states with sales tax, except for Kansas and Missouri, incorporate a marketplace nexus concept into their sales tax laws

  - Often this minimum threshold is the same as the one South Dakota used in the Wayfair decision

    - 200 transactions or $100,000 in sales with a few deviations across the various states

CHAPTER 47

My Lack of Experience With Sales Tax

I'm a NH resident and I currently only sell my books through distributors like Amazon, IngramSpark, Google Play, etc, or through platforms that handle the various taxes for me. Therefore, I've never had to worry about Sales Tax.

But I know that if I were to drive to Massachusetts (creating nexus) for a book signing, I'd have to pay attention to the sales I made during the event, as I could generate both a responsibility to collect and remit **sales taxes** to MA, **but I also might create an <u>income</u> tax nexus.** Which could mean that when I filed my annual taxes on my Form 1040, I'd have to look and see if I have to report income to Massachusetts on a Massachusetts income tax return.

Wait....what?!

Exactly.

Let's talk about **<u>income tax nexus</u>** now...

CHAPTER 48

Income Tax Nexus

So, you drove to another state and made some sales...Or you made a killing on your direct sales website and made $50,000 in sales to someone in State B.

You not only might have 'sales tax nexus' (discussed earlier) but you also might have an *income tax nexus.*

What are income taxes?
- Individuals and businesses are typically required to file annual tax returns, declaring their income and applicable deductions.

- The tax return is used to calculate the amount of tax owed or, in some cases, any refund due.

- **Important note: Just because a company has nexus for sales tax purposes, it does not necessarily mean that they have nexus for income tax purposes**

  ○ Wayfair was a *sales* tax case – not an *income* tax case

  ○ **The requirements for sales tax nexus are not the same as income tax nexus.**

With the exception of a few states, most states require a state income tax return on top of your federal income tax return.
- Boiling it down: If you live and operate your business in State A and have income over XYZ for the year, then you are required to file a State A income tax return as well as your federal income tax return

- However, let's talk about the situations that could require you to file *other* state income tax returns *as well* (think of these three: Property, Payroll, Sales)

  ○ Usually, the presence of property, employees, or other agents who are physically present (on a regular and systematic basis) in State B can mean you might need to file income taxes in State B

(Payroll)

- Generally, you will have income tax nexus when you have an office (or other facilities) in State B *(Property)*

- Usually, if you own or lease equipment in State B, then State B will require an income tax return *(Property)*

- Potentially, if you have inventory (books) waiting to be processed by an unrelated third party in State B *(Property)*

- Usually, if you're in State B soliciting sales *(Sales)*

- Or if you have significant economic activity (Sales) there (Economic Nexus)

  - When a business has significant economic activity within that jurisdiction, regardless of whether it has a physical presence there

    - This concept has become increasingly important with the rise of e-commerce and online business activities.

  - Generally, the business *should* register for business in that 'foreign' state when they have significant economic nexus

    - Research the requirements for the area you are looking at

Have you noticed that I keep saying 'generally,' 'usually,' 'potentially?'

Trust me, it's as frustrating on your CPA's end as it is just reading it here.

There is no hard and fast rule and each state has a different criteria. The kicker: sometimes their criteria is not black and white and explicitly spelled out. **The guidance in the form of case law or statutes detailing the activities that trigger income tax nexus and taxability is lacking in many states.**

For example, one of my CPA Continuing Education classes gave us this statistic: most states say that merely registering with a state agency would not create nexus... but ten states responded that registering with the Secretary of State *would* create nexus. They also said that a small minority of states responded that registration with various agencies *would* cause the business to be subject to tax in their state, while others said that *it did not* create nexus.

Navigating the complexities of nexus can be overwhelming for practitioners and taxpayers, leading to the temptation of assuming universal nexus for every company across all states. However, it's crucial to differentiate between the existence of nexus and the actual obligation to pay taxes. For instance, the presence of a non-sales employee in State A may establish nexus, but the tax implications hinge on various factors. If State A employs a single-factor sales model and the company generates no sales within the state, there might be no obligation to pay income taxes. Filing requirements also depend on factors like exemption thresholds and filing limits.

As I've mentioned many times over (please contact a professional).

CHAPTER 49

*Income Tax Filing Obligations in Other States

Once you determine your company has nexus with a state, it **may** have a filing obligation there.

- **Whether it actually needs to file would depend on the filing thresholds for that state.**

  - *Therefore, you may find that you have significant income tax nexus in a state but you don't hit their threshold for even filing*

  - *These thresholds are so varied that I can't even touch on those here. My best advice is to look it up state by state (I can hear you groaning now. I'm sorry!)*

There are apps or accountants who specialize in tracking and reporting these things (not me!)
- The apps can be plug ins to your website or payment processor

Apportionment factors for income taxes

Assuming that you did reach the state's filing threshold, states use various apportionment factors to determine how much of a business's income is subject to state income tax (when the business operates in multiple states)

These factors help allocate income among different states based on the business's activities within each state. *Most* states do their best to try not to tax the income derived in another state.

Common types of apportionment factors include:
- **Sales Factor:**

  - This factor typically assigns a portion of a business's total income to a state based on the percentage of the company's sales made within that state.

  - It's often weighted heavily in apportioning income.

- **Property Factor:**

  o This factor considers the value of a business's tangible property (such as real estate, inventory, equipment) located in each state compared to the total value of the property.

- **Payroll Factor**

  o It reflects the percentage of a business's total payroll paid to employees working in a particular state compared to the total payroll paid everywhere.

States may use a 'single apportionment factor' or a combination of these factors (above) to determine the portion of a business's income subject to state income tax.

Single Sales Factor:
- Some states use only the sales factor in apportioning income, completely excluding property and payroll factors.

- This approach benefits companies whose sales occur primarily online or across state lines.

Gross Receipts Factor:
- This factor considers a business's gross receipts or total revenue earned within a state compared to the company's total gross receipts.

Cost of Performance:
- In some cases, states use the "cost of performance" method, where income is apportioned based on where the income-producing activity or service is performed.

The specific method and weight given to each factor can vary significantly from state to state, impacting how businesses calculate and apportion their taxable income across different jurisdictions.

Unfortunately, sometimes two states can have unfriendly methods, which can result in a double-taxation of sorts. Most states try to allow for a reduction for the taxes paid to other states, but not all. Consult with your tax professional. I recommend not trying to do this yourself.

CHAPTER 50

*Self-Employment Tax, Qualified Business Income Deduction, and more

This chapter is pretty intense, it's probably best left to a tax professional but just in case you were curious, here's a high-level look.

Self-Employment Taxes

We discussed this briefly earlier, but in case you missed it, be aware that you might owe self-employment (SE) taxes on your author income. Typically, when you are a W2 employee of a company, you pay 50% of the federal payroll taxes, and your employer pays the other 50%, which amounts to 7.65% paid by each of you (for a total of 15.3%)

But when you are self-employed, **you** pay the *employer and employee* portions of Social Security and Medicare taxes.

Social Security Tax:
- The Social Security tax rate is 12.4%, with 6.2% paid by the individual and 6.2% paid by the business.

- However, there is a cap on the income subject to Social Security tax.

Medicare Tax:
- The Medicare tax rate is 2.9%, split equally between the individual and the business.

- Unlike Social Security tax, there is no income cap for Medicare tax.

This 15.3% of self-employment tax is calculated on your business income, *on top of your ordinary income tax rate also being applied to it.*

This calculation of self-employment taxes is calculated at the same time as you prepare your Form 1040 personal income tax return.

Unlike traditional employees who have taxes withheld from their paychecks, self-employed individuals are responsible for making quarterly estimated tax payments to cover both income and self-employment taxes.

To mitigate the impact of self-employment tax, authors can explore deductions related to their business expenses, home office deductions, and other eligible costs.

Form 1040 (2023)				Page 2
Tax and Credits	16	**Tax** (see instructions). Check if any from Form(s): 1 ☐ 8814 2 ☐ 4972 3 ☐ _____	16	
	17	Amount from Schedule 2, line 3	17	
	18	Add lines 16 and 17	18	
	19	Child tax credit or credit for other dependents from Schedule 8812	19	
	20	Amount from Schedule 3, line 8	20	
	21	Add lines 19 and 20	21	
	22	Subtract line 21 from line 18. If zero or less, enter -0-	22	
	23	Other taxes, including self-employment tax, from Schedule 2, line 21	23	
	24	Add lines 22 and 23. This is your **total tax**	24	

Self-employment taxes on your Form 1040 tax return.

See how it's computed separately from ordinary income tax and how they get added together to figure the Total Tax.

This is the part that is hard for self-employed individuals to remember: you might make money on your writing business, but maybe your spouse had enough losses on his business to net against it that your joint taxable income is actually zero (or less)...

You still owe self-employment taxes on that self employment income.

Please remember this when you are doing your planning.

Say that you have a writer business that reports on your Schedule C but your spouse owns a separate Schedule C business. For the sake of small, easy numbers, let's say that you made $10,000 net income in your author business, but your spouse had a net loss of $10,000 in their business. That nets to zero for your joint taxable income, right? For the sake of simplicity, we're going to say yes, but even though you had a net zero joint taxable income for the year, the IRS still sees that you *made* $10,000 in your author business, so you know what that means....taxes. So yes, even though jointly you had a zero balance total income on your tax return, you still made self-employment income before your spouse's loss offset it, which means you need to pay that 15.3% tax on that. You won't have ordinary income tax because of that zero total income number, but that SE tax? Yup, still there, even if you don't owe income tax.

It will trip self-employed owners up every time. Please keep that in mind.

One small blessing in all this that makes it feel like you're not getting kicked square in the teeth?

The **self-employment (SE) tax deduction** is a provision that allows self-employed individuals to deduct a portion of their self-employment taxes when calculating their adjusted gross income (AGI). Basically, you get to take 50% of whatever your SE tax is, and deduct it on your Form 1040 tax return income to reduce the number on which your ordinary income tax calculation is based.

The deduction is made with pretax dollars, so it's not a 1:1 savings, but you at least get to take *something*.

In the scenario above, it wouldn't help much, because your taxable income for the year was already at zero and it can't be reduced further than that, but when you don't have that offsetting loss, it's nice to be able to take at least something and get some sort of benefit for the SE tax you need to pay (even if it's not quite as beneficial as deducting actual payroll taxes like an actual employer would be able to). Please note, this deduction does not affect the amount of SE tax owed, it just potentially reduces the ordinary income tax owed.

Schedule 1 (Form 1040) 2023			Page **2**
Part II	**Adjustments to Income**		
11	Educator expenses	11	
12	Certain business expenses of reservists, performing artists, and fee-basis government officials. Attach Form 2106	12	
13	Health savings account deduction. Attach Form 8889	13	
14	Moving expenses for members of the Armed Forces. Attach Form 3903	14	
15	Deductible part of self-employment tax. Attach Schedule SE	15	
16	Self-employed SEP, SIMPLE, and qualified plans	16	
17	Self-employed health insurance deduction	17	
18	Penalty on early withdrawal of savings	18	
19a	Alimony paid	19a	
b	Recipient's SSN		
c	Date of original divorce or separation agreement (see instructions): _____		
20	IRA deduction	20	

See Line 15 where the SE tax deduction goes.

You can also see where retirement contributions go.

Let's talk about another deduction that can reduce ordinary income tax...

Self-Employed Health Insurance Deduction

The self-employed health insurance deduction is a tax benefit that allows self-employed individuals to deduct the cost of health insurance premiums from their income when calculating their adjusted gross income (AGI).

Self-employed individuals who meet certain criteria can deduct the premiums paid for health, dental, and qualified long-term care insurance coverage **for themselves, their spouses, and their dependents.**

This deduction is available for individuals who are self-employed and report their business income on Schedule C, Schedule C-EZ, or Schedule F. Note – you can only take this deduction up to the extent you have a profit on your business return.

There are a few rules to make sure you qualify but at a high level: 1) you cannot be eligible to participate in a subsidized health plan through an employer's plan or your spouse's employer's plan, and 2) the deduction is not available for any month in which you are eligible to participate in any subsidized health plan maintained by your employer, your spouse, or any dependent.

It boils down to this: Self-employed individuals can usually claim the deduction when completing their individual income tax return (Form 1040). The deduction is taken currently on Schedule 1, page 2, reducing the individual's total income. By deducting health insurance premiums, self-employed individuals can lower their AGI, potentially reducing their overall ordinary income tax liability.

See image above for location.

Qualified Business Income Deduction

As an author managing your own business, you may benefit from a tax deduction known as the Qualified Business Income (QBI) deduction (Section 199A deduction). This deduction allows eligible businesses to deduct a portion of their 'qualified business income' when calculating their taxable income. This is a relatively new deduction and is set to expire after 2025 – but tax laws change all the time, so please double check the current applicability of this section at the time of your reading (that should actually be done for all of the passages in this book. Double check applicability for everything, because, *remember, this isn't tax advice* :-)).

This is an *ADVANCED tax discussion so I'm not going to go into crazy detail here – talk to a professional in your area who can customize their explanation in the context of your business.*

The QBI deduction is generally available to individuals, including authors, who operate as pass-through entities such as sole proprietorships, single-member LLCs, partnerships, S corporations, trust, or estates.

The deduction is calculated based on a percentage (up to 20%) of your qualified business income, which includes income from your writing activities and related business endeavors.

There are certain limitations and phase-out thresholds based on your total income, filing status, and the type of business you operate.

- Per the IRS: "The QBI Component is subject to limitations, depending on the taxpayer's taxable income which may include the type of trade or business, the amount of W-2 wages paid by the qualified trade or business, and the unadjusted basis immediately after acquisition (UBIA) of qualified property held by the trade or business."

- You might hear the phrase SSTB – which is a Specified Service Trade or Business. I'm of the current belief that authors fall into the SSTB category. You probably don't have to do anything with this information. If you have a preparer, they'll take care of how the QBI deduction is applied (or not applied) to your tax return.

Given the complexities and variations in tax laws, especially in relation to QBI, it's advisable to consult with a tax professional who can provide personalized guidance based on your specific situation.

jointly or Qualifying surviving spouse, $27,700	8	Additional income from Schedule 1, line 10	8	
	9	Add lines 1z, 2b, 3b, 4b, 5b, 6b, 7, and 8. This is your **total income**	9	
• Head of household, $20,800	10	Adjustments to income from Schedule 1, line 26	10	
• If you checked any box under *Standard Deduction,* see instructions.	11	Subtract line 10 from line 9. This is your **adjusted gross income**	11	
	12	**Standard deduction or itemized deductions** (from Schedule A)	12	
	13	Qualified business income deduction from Form 8995 or Form 8995-A	13	
	14	Add lines 12 and 13	14	
	15	Subtract line 14 from line 11. If zero or less, enter -0-. This is your **taxable income**	15	

For Disclosure, Privacy Act, and Paperwork Reduction Act Notice, see separate instructions.   Cat. No. 11320B   Form **1040** (2023)

See where the QBI Deduction appears on Line 13 of Form 1040 and how it's used to compute Total Income

CHAPTER 51

Contractors vs. employees

Understanding the distinction between contractors and employees is crucial for any author managing a growing business.

This chapter delves into the key differences and the implications they hold for your financial and legal responsibilities. Especially if you hire virtual assistants or personal assistants in the course of your author business. VA's often tend to be contractors; PAs...well, they usually have a closer relationship with the owner, have more predictable schedules, have no end date, maybe have access to log-ins or other software... Maybe they'd be an employee... Take a look at the structure of their responsibilities and make that decision for yourself.

Contractors

Work Relationship:
- Contractors are typically self-employed individuals or businesses that offer services to other businesses.

- They operate independently and provide services under a contract or agreement.
  - They are usually hired for specific projects or durations

Control and Independence:
- Contractors have more control over how they perform their work.

- They control their schedules, methods, tools used, and might work for multiple clients simultaneously.

Payment and Taxes:
- Contractors are responsible for paying their taxes, including self-employment taxes (Social Security and Medicare), and often invoice the business for their services.

- They receive a Form 1099-NEC if their payments exceed $600 in a tax year.

Benefits and Protections:
- Independent contractors generally don't receive employee benefits such as health insurance, retirement plans, or paid leave.

- They're not covered by employment laws like minimum wage or overtime pay.

Employees

Work Relationship:
- Employees work under the direction and control of the employer.

- They perform tasks assigned by the employer and are part of the company's regular operations.

Control and Supervision:
- Employers have more control over employees' work, including work hours, methods, and tools used.

- Employees often work exclusively for their employer.

Payment and Taxes:
- Employers withhold income taxes, Social Security, and Medicare taxes from employee paychecks.

- Employees receive a Form W-2 at the end of the year detailing their earnings.

Benefits and Protections:
- Employees are eligible for various benefits, including health insurance, retirement plans, paid leave, workers' compensation, and protection under employment laws for minimum wage, overtime pay, and workplace safety.

Implications of Misclassification:
1. **Legal Ramifications:**

   ○ Misclassifying workers can lead to legal repercussions, including fines and back taxes.

- Understanding the criteria for each classification is paramount.

2. **Tax Obligations:**

- Different tax withholding rules apply to employees and contractors.

- Comprehending these distinctions helps in accurate tax reporting and compliance.

Guidelines for Correct Classification:
1. IRS Guidelines:

- Familiarize yourself with the IRS guidelines on worker classification.

- These guidelines provide clear criteria for distinguishing between employees and contractors.

2. Documentation:

- Maintain detailed records of agreements, project scopes, and payment structures.

- Clear documentation supports the proper classification of workers.

It might be more appealing for you to not have to worry about calculating, withholding, remitting, and filing payroll taxes. You might also not want to deal with adding them to your retirement plan, or offering different benefits. The costs are usually much smaller with paying someone as a contractor.

But understanding and navigating the contractor-employee classification is an essential necessity for authors managing a team. Don't play with the rules – the penalties are rough.

Review, structure and document the work terms explicitly so there is backup available if the arrangement were ever challenged.

CHAPTER 52

Copyrights

Copyright is a legal right that grants authors exclusive control over their original works, protecting them from unauthorized use or reproduction.

It covers literary, artistic, musical, or other creative works, including books, manuscripts, novels, and digital content.

In most countries, including the US, your work is automatically copyrighted upon creation and fixation in a tangible medium (like writing your book).

However, registering your copyright with the U.S. Copyright Office provides additional legal benefits and proof of ownership in case of infringement. Luckily, you no longer have to send in physical copies to complete the copyright – electronic versions are sufficient.

Copyright allows authors to reproduce, distribute, display, and create derivative works based on their original creation. It lasts for the author's lifetime plus 70 years in the US (duration varies in other countries) (though there are different rules for publishing with a pen name)

Unsolicited, non-legal tip: From every attorney I've ever spoken with – don't include lyrics of songs that don't belong to you in your work. You can reference the song title, but don't include the lyrics.

CHAPTER 53

Vanity publishers

This doesn't really fall into the category of bookkeeping or tax advice...or maybe it does.... But from a business advising standpoint, be wary of vanity publishers.

What is a vanity publisher?

Unlike traditional publishers who usually cover the costs and take on the financial risk of publishing a book, **a vanity publisher requires the author to pay for various publishing services, like editing, design, printing, and distribution. Then they publish the book themselves, collecting the royalties and then remitting an agreed-upon amount to the author.**

Vanity publishers tend to focus more on making money from the author rather than on the book's success in the market.

If you have to pay for all of that stuff to be done - pause, research, and don't make any rash decisions. Look up the company and proceed with caution. A simple search online or in any of the writers' groups will usually give you first-hand experiences and warnings on whether or not it's legitimate.

I think the general consensus is: if the publisher is asking you to pay for those things...you maybe should just self-publish

My point here is just to exercise caution when approached with terms similar to those that I outlined above.

Chapter 54

ISBN (International Standard Book Number)

An ISBN is a unique numeric identifier assigned to each edition and variation of a book, used for cataloging, ordering, and identifying books globally.

It's crucial for book distribution, library acquisitions, and tracking sales data.

Each format (hardcover, paperback, ebook, audiobook) and edition of a book should have its own ISBN.

In the US, ISBNs are obtained through Bowker, the official ISBN agency (be wary of other sites trying to sell you ISBNs).

They can be purchased individually or in bulk for multiple titles.

The ISBN is typically found on the copyright page of a book, facilitating easy identification and sales tracking.

Some distributors will offer your their own ISBN for 'free' but you can't publish that particular ISBN elsewhere. That doesn't necessarily mean you can't publish the *book* elsewhere though. Usually that just means that 'that' ISBN can't be used to create that format book at another printer/distributor. If you use ABC's ISBN for a paperback but want to also have your paperback listed through XYZ, that's usually fine. You just need a different ISBN for the one sold through XYZ. Check the fine print.

Fun fact: ISBNs are (as of this writing) free in Canada, Australia, New Zealand, and some European countries (e.g. Germany and France)

CHAPTER 55

Lower your tax prep bill

I frequently get asked what a business owner can do to reduce their tax prep bill.

This is what I usually suggest:

- Give your materials to the preparer all at once rather than piecemeal

- Give a copy of your QuickBooks file to the preparer, rather than printed out pages from your QB file

  - Or give them Accountant's access if you use QuickBooks Online or another online bookkeeping platform

  - Remember to give them passwords for logins

- Have a clean Chart of Accounts and TB

  - Don't have an account for 'wages' and then another for 'salaries'

  - Don't have separate accounts for: electricity, heat, oil, internet, gas, oil, etc

    - They can all just be lumped together in 'utilities'

- Make sure you had added the adjusting journal entries that the tax preparer made during the prior year's tax prep

- If you're a paper ledger person and keep track of your finances on paper trackers, figure out the subtotals for each tax line item yourself

- Don't give them receipts unless they ask for them

- Keep track of your mileage in a log throughout the year

- *Don't* staple your documents together

- Use my year-end tax checklist to make sure you give them the entire package of information

CHAPTER 56
What I can do for you

- I've created an **Essential Year-End Tax Checklist for Authors**

  - It reminds you of all of the items that your tax preparer may ask for during tax prep so you can compile them ahead of time, preventing headache-inducing back-and-forth questions for both you (and your CPA). *Trust me. Been there. We as CPAs want the information all at once. The fewer times we have to go back and forth with the client...the better.*

    - *Free with a newsletter sign-up*

- I created a paper journal tracker called the **Bookkeeping Organizer for Authors**

  - It's a log book that boils down the bookkeeping piece and allows for more organized records and a more seamless tax prep in an non-overwhelming way. It allows you to record your income and expenses in a brilliantly organized manner, allowing for monthly subtotal summaries which will then be added up at year-end into the yearly totals that you would use for tax prep. It's gorgeous. For planner people who love the tactile touch of paper – *it's a beauty.*

- I created **The Ultimate Income and Expense Excel Tracker** that authors can use to track their income and expenses in a foolproof manner.

  - This masterpiece of an Excel file not only tracks your income and expenses, but has a spot for mileage and for home office too.

  - *It also automatically computes monthly income-to-expense comparisons and populates a rough draft of your Schedule C tax return*

  - A one-off, small investment for years of use and countless headaches avoided.

    - It doesn't offer the same automation as a software that allows for bank feeds to be synced in, but it's still easier than a paper log book.

- I've created an **Author's Business and Financial Handbook: Tips for Bookkeeping, Accounting, and Taxes**

- ○ *This tome – thanks for buying!*

- **I offer custom QuickBooks Online set-ups**

  - ○ I can help you custom set-up your own QBO account, including the-set up of bank feeds to <u>automate</u> your bookkeeping as much as possible.

    - Your time is valuable. Spend it writing rather than record-keeping. Leave the bookkeeping to the software

- **Webinars**: And I've created **a series of webinars to coach you on handling your author business.** The videos range from basic concepts to more complex (What is an LLC? How do I read the statements? How do I keep track of my records? What can I deduct and where? How can I set up my own QBO file for world domination and precise pen name/series/book profitability tracking for more strategic decision making. What does direct sales mean from an accountant's perspective? Etc.)

CHAPTER 57

Glossary

- **Balance Sheet**:

    ○ A financial statement that shows a company's assets, liabilities, and equity at a specific point in time, providing a snapshot of its financial position.

- **Income Statement / Profit and Loss Statement:**

    ○ A financial statement that shows a company's revenues, expenses, and net income over a specific period, usually a month, quarter, or year.

- **Cash Flow Statement**:

    ○ A financial statement that shows how changes in balance sheet accounts and income affect cash

    ○ Provides insight into a company's operating, investing, and financing activities.

- **Assets**:

    ○ Resources owned by a business, including cash, inventory, property, equipment, and accounts receivable.

- **Liabilities**:

    ○ Debts or obligations owed by a business to creditors, including accounts payable, loans, and mortgages.

- **Equity**:

    ○ The residual interest in the assets of a business after deducting liabilities; it represents the owners' or shareholders' stake in the company.

- **Accounts Payable (AP):**

    ○ Money owed by a business to its suppliers or vendors for goods or services purchased on credit.

- **Accounts Receivable (AR):**

  - Money owed to a business by its customers for goods or services provided on credit.

- **Debits and Credits:**

  - The system used in double-entry bookkeeping where debits represent the left side and credits represent the right side of an accounting entry.

- **General Ledger:**

  - A complete record of all financial transactions of a business, organized by accounts.

- **Trial Balance:**

  - A list of all general ledger accounts with their balances to ensure that the debits equal the credits.

- **Net Income:**

  - The difference between a company's total revenue and total expenses, also known as the bottom line or profit.

- **Gross Profit:**

  - Revenue minus the cost of goods sold, representing the profit before deducting operating expenses.

- **Accrual Basis Accounting:**

  - Recording revenues and expenses when they are earned or incurred, regardless of when cash changes hands.

- **Cash Basis Accounting:**

  - Recording revenues and expenses only when cash is received or paid.

- **Depreciation:**

  - Allocating the cost of a tangible asset over its useful life to accurately reflect its diminishing value.

- **Chart of Accounts:**

  - A list of all the accounts used by a business, organized in a structured manner to categorize transactions.

www.ingramcontent.com/pod-product-compliance
Lightning Source LLC
Chambersburg PA
CBHW052112020426

42335CB00021B/2731